D0475817

RUGBY
HAS
F★★★ING
LAWS
NOT
RULES

RUGBY HAS F★★★ING LAWS NOT RULES

A GUIDED TOUR THROUGH RUGBY'S BIZARRE LAW BOOK

PAUL WILLIAMS

POLARIS
PUBLISHING

This edition first published in 2021 by

POLARIS PUBLISHING LTD
c/o Aberdein Considine
2nd Floor, Elder House
Multrees Walk
Edinburgh
EH1 3DX

Distributed by
Birlinn Limited

www.polarispublishing.com

Text copyright © Paul Williams, 2021

ISBN: 9781913538668
eBook ISBN: 9781913538675

3

The right of Paul Williams to be identified as the author of this work has been
asserted by him in accordance with the Copyright, Designs and Patents Act 1988.

All rights reserved. No part of this publication may be reproduced, stored
or transmitted in any form, or by any means electronic, mechanical, photocopying,
recording or otherwise, without the express written permission of the publisher.

The views expressed in this book do not necessarily reflect the views, opinions or policies of Polaris Publishing Ltd (Company
No. SC401508) (Polaris), nor those of any persons, organisations or commercial partners connected with the same
(Connected Persons). Any opinions, advice, statements, services, offers, or other information or content expressed by third
parties are not those of Polaris or any Connected Persons but those of the third parties. For the avoidance of doubt, neither
Polaris nor any Connected Persons assume any responsibility or duty of care whether contractual, delictual or on any other
basis towards any person in respect of any such matter and accept no liability for any loss or damage caused by any such
matter in this book.

Every effort has been made to trace copyright holders and obtain their permission for the use of copyright material.
The publisher apologises for any errors or omissions and would be grateful if notified of any corrections that should be
incorporated in future reprints or editions of this book.

British Library Cataloguing-in-Publication Data
A catalogue record for this book is available on request from the British Library.

Designed and typeset by Polaris Publishing, Edinburgh
Printed in Great Britain by CPI Group (UK) Ltd, Croydon, CR0 4YY

Thanks to my wife, parents, brother and two
beautiful children, Chloe and Rosie.
They put up with a lot of rugby.

ABOUT THE AUTHOR

Paul Williams is a columnist for the United Rugby Championship website and *Rugby World* magazine.

A once tackle-shy second row, he has a deep love of attacking flair, questionable clothing and low-calorie lager. He lives in Cardiff.

CONTENTS

INTRODUCTION

Much like a drug-addicted model from the 1990s, rugby is beautiful but complicated. So complicated, that before you even begin to understand the reams of rules, some absolute penis will usually tell you that they're not even called rules. Yes, rugby has laws, not rules – something that the smuggest of rugby aficionados will usually mention within 1.4 seconds of discussing how the game is refereed. But this finickity need to differentiate the fact that rugby has laws, not rules, isn't merely used as an academic point. More often it's used as a verbal landmine to place in front of unsuspecting supporters, newcomers to the game and, in particular, football fans (the pleasure of verbally maiming football fans is a source of much pleasure to some rugby fans).

This oral disembowelment isn't just reserved for football fans, of course. Even diehard, lifelong rugby fans occasionally call them rules, not laws, and there's no exemption for them either. No sooner has the faux pas been made than rugby's gallows are erected and you're left swinging as the angry crowds jeer. However, learning what rugby's legislative procedures are called is the easy bit – there are only two options after all. But once you've got that bit right, it's into the laws themselves. Laws that have so many interpretations and combinations that it was rumoured to be the subject of the late Stephen Hawking's final book.

P.S. This is a very light-hearted look at rugby and is by no means a slight on the laws, the people who play by them or referee them. Especially those who referee them. Rugby is the hardest sport in the world to officiate and the author would rather eat a cold shit pie than even attempt to referee a senior game of rugby, such is the difficulty. Hats off to all referees who keep this great game on the straight and narrow.

'The key to understanding rugby's laws
is knowing that you never truly will.'
Plato

GLOSSARY

22: The gap between the goal line and the 22-metre line. Or if you're in your mid-40s, the 25-yard line, which many still get confused, even though it changed about 95 years ago. These are the same people who eat Opal Fruits and Marathons.

A

Actual time: Time elapsed – the time on the clock, which depending on fitness levels can feel like 80 minutes or two decades. The starting of that period of time is usually announced with a whistle. The end of that period of time is also delineated with a whistle, plus sometimes the sound of relief, crying and/or vomiting.

Advantage: A tactical or territorial benefit arising after an infringement – a period that refuses to fit in with the space-time continuum and is entirely dependent on how a referee feels that day. Could be a few seconds. Could be enough for a new species to evolve on the pitch right in front of the supporters' eyes.

Attacking team: The team with the ball – whether they choose to genuinely attack or put up another fucking box-kick is a different matter altogether.

B

Ball-carrier: A player in possession of the ball – the whole point of rugby, unless you're a modern Test coach and believe that the sky should have higher possession stats than your players.

Beyond or behind or in front of a position: Must be with both feet except where that isn't possible – doesn't apply to scrum-halves apparently, who do what they like, when they like.

Binding: Grasping another player's body firmly between the shoulders and the hips with the whole arm in contact – think of *Dirty Dancing*, with more aggression but worse footwork.

Blood injury: Uncontrolled active bleeding – a wonderful term that conjures images of 18th century Parisian fountains gushing with an endless supply of rugby players' blood.

C

Captain: The player nominated by a team to lead that team and consult the referee. At professional level, it can also be the one who is best at the media duties. At amateur level, it's the player who cares enough to chase up players midweek, knowing there's a cold snap coming and some players won't fancy travelling three hours on a bus only to lose the match, and possibly some of their fingers to frostbite. Also, the player who collects valuables before kick-off, often in a sock or woolly hat.

Cavalry charge: An illegal type of attack – usually happens near the goal line when the attacking team is awarded a penalty or free kick. At a signal from the kicker, a line of attacking players charges forward from a distance. When they get near, the kicker taps the ball and passes to a player – one of the most beautiful and dangerous things you'll ever see. Imagine Sofía Vergara with her hands dipped in melted resin and broken glass. Fantastic to admire from a distance, but if you get too close, you'll get messed up.

D

Dead: The ball is dead when the referee blows the whistle to stop play or following an unsuccessful conversion – an unusually morbid term for a very innocent act. It's like calling the lineout a death corridor.

Dead-ball line: The line at either end (and not part) of the playing area. Death seems to be a recurring feature in rugby terminology – no one really knows why.

Directly caught: A ball caught without first touching anyone else/the ground – weirdly complicated. Just means someone caught the ball.

Drop-kick: After being intentionally dropped to the ground from the hand or hands, the ball is kicked as it rises from its first bounce – one of the most underrated skills in the world, not just rugby. A kick that relies on the bounce of a ball that simply won't do what it's told. Rugby balls are compulsive liars and should be treated as such.

F

Field of play: The area between the goal lines and the touchlines. Those lines are not part of the field of play – again overly complicated. It means the rugby pitch on which you're playing. It's like telling you that you're reading right now. Which you are.

Flying wedge: An illegal type of attack, which usually happens near the goal line when the attacking team is awarded a penalty or free kick. The kicker taps the ball and starts the attack, either by driving towards the goal line or by passing to a team-mate, who drives forward. Immediately, team-mates bind on each side of the ball-carrier in a wedge formation before engaging the opposition. Often one or more of these team-mates is in front of the ball-carrier – much like the death penalty and national service, it's something that many would love to see brought back, but law makers simply won't agree to ratify the level of gratuitous violence that the public loves so much.

Forward: Towards the opposition's dead-ball line – or asking another player if they would like to have sex with you there and then.

Foul play: Anything a player does within the playing enclosure that's contrary to Law 9 governing – fucking up and getting caught.

Free kick: Awarded against a team for an infringement or to a team for a mark – a sort of diet penalty.

G

Goal: The ball is place-kicked or drop-kicked over the opponents' crossbar from the field of play – the total opposite of a goal in football.

Goal line: The line at either end (and not part) of the field of play – the thing that looks like a massive line of cocaine and delivers a similar buzz when you touch it.

(the) Ground: The total area shown in the ground diagram in Law 1 – the floor and stuff to do with the floor. It's a floor-related subject.

H

Half-time: The interval between the two halves of the game. The bit where you can sit down and stop crying – whether a supporter or player. Used to be a time for players to digest half an orange. Now they digest PowerPoint slides and swear words from their defence coach.

Hand-off: A permitted action, taken by a ball-carrier to fend off an opponent, using the palm of the hand – it's like punching someone in the face, but without having to go to court and explain yourself.

Hindmost: Nearest a team's own goal line – a bizarre word from medieval times that no one uses any more.

Holding the ball: Being in possession of the ball in the hand or hands or in the arm or arms – if you need this explained to, you're doing very well to be reading and breathing at the same time.

I

In-goal: The area between the goal line and dead-ball line, and between the touch-in-goal lines. It includes the goal line but not the dead-ball line or the touch-in-goal lines – the bit where you score tries or where cocky players get caught with the ball doing stupid things – usually flankers who wanted to be backs, or the substitute outside-half trying to impress. If you're the defending team, nothing good ever comes from being behind your own goal line.

Infield: Within the playing area, away from the touchlines – the bits inside the lines. Also, a very good name for a rugby boy band. 'Welcome to the stage, Infield!' Out runs the scrum-half, the outside-half, the outside-centre – and possibly a prop for equality reasons.

J
Jersey: A shirt worn on the upper half of the body and which isn't attached to shorts or underwear – this rule basically explains that a jersey isn't a onesie.

K
Kick: An act made by intentionally hitting the ball with any part of the leg or foot, except the heel, from

the toe to the knee but not including the knee. A kick must move the ball a visible distance out of the hand or along the ground – 'to kick' as in to kick-the-bucket, something that has ironically happened to passing and running, thanks to kicking.

Kick-off: The method of starting each half of a match and at the beginning of each period of extra time with a drop-kick. The start of 80 minutes of pure joy or misery.

Kicked directly into touch: The ball is kicked into touch without first landing on the playing area or touching a player or the referee – more difficult than it looks or sounds.

Kicking tee: Any device approved by the match organiser to support the ball when taking a place-kick – small, plastic, doesn't fly through the air as well as you would think it would. Replaced sand and mud in the 1990s – only on the rugby field, of course. Otherwise, beaches and face-packs would be very different and unpleasant scenarios.

Knock-on: When a player loses possession of the ball and it goes forward, or when a player hits the ball forward with the hand or arm, or when the ball hits the hand or arm and goes forward and the ball touches the ground or another player before the original player can catch it. It's always the fault of the player catching, never the player passing. The opposite situation occurs at lineouts, where the hooker, who essentially passes the ball, must take the blame regardless.

L

Line of touch: At amateur level, the line of touch separates those people who have a pint in their hand and those who don't. Also separates those who play the game and those who have opinions on the game.

Line through the mark or place: Unless stated otherwise, a line parallel to the touchline – mystical lines that don't mean much to anyone except referees. Very similar to the Nazca lines in South America.

Lineout: A lineout is a set piece consisting of a line of at least two players from each team waiting to receive a throw from touch – it's where centres, who have converted to hooker, finally get shown up for the con artists that they are.

Lineout players: The players in either line of a lineout – very similar in appearance to the line-up at an eat-as-much-as-you-like buffet. Very, very similar. In many ways.

Mark: A method of suspending play and winning a free kick by directly catching an opponent's kick in the catcher's own 22 or in-goal and shouting 'mark' – one of the key reasons why people named Mark have historically avoided watching live rugby. And those that do take Valium.

Mark of touch: An imaginary line in the field of play at right angles to the touchline through the place where the ball is thrown in. The mark of touch can't be within five metres of a goal line – the straight line along which hookers are supposed to throw the ball. Any wind over 15mph renders this impossible and you may as well be throwing feathers down a wind tunnel.

Match officials: Those who control the game, usually consisting of a referee and two assistant referees or touch judges but may also include a television match official and, in sevens, two in-goal judges. The folks with the flags and whistles who do a ridiculously complicated job that simply can't be completed unless you have compound eyes, like a fly. Also double up as emotional sponges to suck up the hatred that has built up from people during the week.

Match organiser: Administrative body responsible for the match, which may be World Rugby, a union, a group of unions or any organisation approved by a union or World Rugby – the people in power. Power level varies from three people drinking tea while sitting around a table in a shed, to 20 people sitting around a table made from the bones of snow tigers, while drinking chilled swans' blood.

Maul: A phase of play consisting of a ball-carrier and at least one player from each team, bound together and on their feet – the anaconda of rugby. Slow, but effective at killing stuff.

N

Near: Within one metre – bet you didn't know near meant this in rugby, did you?

O

Obstruction: When a player attempting to play is illegally impeded and prevented from doing so – often done by a player who believes they have temporarily become invisible to the human eye.

Off feet: Players are off their feet when any other part of the body is supported by the ground or players on the ground – unless you're an openside from the opposing team, where you're reclassified as a millipede that can't ever be off its feet unless it's on its back.

Offside: A positional offence meaning a player can take no part in the game without being liable to sanction – an area of the world where Australians believe New Zealanders live.

On feet: Players are on their feet if no other part of their body is supported by the ground or players on the ground – doesn't apply to some opensides, whose feet count as hands and vice versa. In rugby terms, opensides are often considered quadrupedal, like a dog or cat. They will also sometimes urinate on things to signify ownership.

Open play: The period after a kick-off, restart kick, free kick, penalty or set piece and before the next phase, or the period between phases of play, excluding when the ball is dead. The good bit.

P

Participating players at a lineout: These consist of lineout players, one receiver from each team (if present), the player who throws in and an immediate opponent. Often tall, wide or both. On occasion you'll find a back standing in there, but they look like a Tory MP at an LGBT march – clearly out of place.

Pass: A player throws or hands the ball to another player. Can be a beautiful spiral pass that pushes physics to its limits or it can be a deliberate end-on pass – ugly but practical in its application. Passing is what separates good centres from great centres.

Penalty: Awarded against a team for a serious infringement. If your mother or father ever gave you a clip round the ear, it's rugby's equivalent of that.

Penalty try: Awarded when, in the opinion of the

referee, a try probably would have been scored (or scored in a more advantageous position) if not for an act of foul play by an opponent. The ultimate insult. It basically means that your team is so bad at rugby that we're not even going to go through the motions. The other team is going to score at some point so we might as well cut to the chase and get it over with.

Phase of play: Scrum, lineout, ruck or maul. Often followed by a fucking box-kick.

Place-kick: The ball is kicked after it has been placed on the ground (or on an approved kicking tee) for that purpose. Rugby's version of putting in golf. A sport within a sport. Often executed by number 10s and 15s in many countries. Except in France, where it's still the domain of scrum-halves.

Placer: A player holding the ball for a team-mate to place-kick. Usually reserved for windy days in modern rugby or poorly built mounds in the old days. Normally executed by the player with the lowest IQ in the team and to whom a swift kick to the head wouldn't cause any immediately obvious ramifications.

Plane of touch: The vertical space rising immediately above the touch line or touch-in-goal line. Sounds like an 80s album title but is actually the bit where the ball crosses the line.

Played: The ball is played when it's intentionally touched by a player. Alternatively, it's where your team ended up signing a player who turns out to be shit.

Players' clothing: Anything players wear, which, to be legal, must conform to World Rugby regulation. Doesn't include the clothing they wear after the game, but it should. The standard of sartorial matters in most rugby clubs needs attention. Haircuts should also be part of this new disciplinary commission, particularly those in rural New Zealand and Exeter.

Playing time: Actual time, excluding time lost for stoppages. The longer the better, unless you're a prop.

Possession: An individual or team in control of the ball or who are attempting to bring it under control. Nine-tenths of the law apparently, but if you have a good defence coach your team may be happy with about six-ninths.

Punt: A player intentionally drops the ball and kicks it before it touches the ground. Or, attempting to convert a rugby league player to union 12 months before a Rugby World Cup.

Q

Quick throw: A throw from touch taken before the lineout is formed. The ball is thrown in by the team that would have thrown the ball into the lineout. Fantastic for counter-attacking or getting absolutely smashed by a player on a 30-yard run-up.

R

Receiver: The player in a position to receive the ball if it's knocked or passed back from a lineout. Usually the scrum-half and usually talking shit.

Red card: The card shown by the referee to a player to indicate that they have been permanently excluded from the match. Rugby's public gallows, which often receive the same level of groans and snarls from the crowd.

Replacement: A player who replaces a team-mate because of injury or for tactical reasons. At elite level, a player of roughly the same ability. At lower levels, usually means swapping a rugby player for anything else that was available walking near the clubhouse.

Restart kick: The method of restarting play with a drop-kick after a score or a touchdown. The bread and butter of outside-halves. Much like flatpack furniture, it sounds easy but isn't at all.

Ruck: A phase of play where one or more players from each team who are on their feet and in physical contact, close around the ball, which is on the ground. If you've ever looked through a microscope at a petri dish of germs and bacteria frantically running around in chaotic directions, it's like that.

Rucking: Legally using one's feet to try to win or keep possession of the ball in a ruck. In the modern era it means playing the ball with your feet. Twenty years ago, rucking was something very different. It meant using the studs of your boots to remove the opposition players from the ruck, like a nit comb removing head lice.

S

Sanction: The method by which the game is restarted following an infringement or stoppage. The punishment for being a naughty boy or girl.

Scrum: A set piece, normally consisting of eight players from each team bound together in formation. One of the natural world's most wonderous sights. Ranks alongside wildebeest migrating and the murmuration of birds.

Sent off: A player is shown a red card and is permanently excluded from the match. Used to be a once-in-a-career situation. Now, with player safety rightly a priority, players see more red than a sommelier.

Shorts: Trousers that start at the waist and end above the knees, have an elasticated waistband and/or drawstring, and are not attached to the jersey or underwear. A visual aid to spot those who skip leg day.

Sin-bin: The designated place outside the playing area within which a temporarily suspended player must remain. A reinforced naughty step.

Stiff-arm tackle: An illegal tackle whereby a player uses a stiff arm to strike the ball-carrier. Rarely seen or heard of anymore. There are so many other ways to get sent off that the stiff arm simply isn't required.

T

Tackle: The method of holding a ball-carrier and bringing that player to ground. What separates proper rugby players from those who simply like catching and running with the ball.

Tackled player: A ball-carrier who is held and taken to ground by a tackler or tacklers. Person on the floor questioning why they're not at home, in the warm, with a brew.

Tackler: An opposition player who holds the tackled player and goes to ground. Person who put the person mentioned above on the floor.

Team-mate: Another player of the same team. Way more than just another player of the same team . . . they're your friends off the field, often for life.

Temporarily suspended: Excluded from the game for a specified period of playing time, usually ten minutes. Rugby's version of parole.

Throw forward: When a player throws or passes the ball forward, i.e. if the arms of the player passing the ball move forward. Sounds simple but remains one of the great debates in modern physics.

Touch: The area alongside the field of play that includes the touchlines and beyond. Like the outskirts of a rough city, best avoided if possible. If you must go there, take others with you.

Touch-in-goal: The area alongside the in-goal area that includes the touch-in-goal lines and beyond. One of the areas of the pitch that thinks it's more important than it really is.

U

Uncontested scrum: A scrum in which the team throwing in gains possession without contest, with neither team being allowed to push from the mark – looks a bit like a normal scrum in rugby league.

Underwear: An undergarment that covers the body from the waist, having short or no legs, ending above the knees, and is worn next to the skin or under clothing, and isn't attached to the jersey or shorts – seems bizarre that rugby needs to define underwear but there we are. I don't know what else to tell you. Boots, hair, eyes and skin are not defined, but underpants are. Strange.

Union: A body, approved by World Rugby, responsible for the organising and playing of games within a specific geographical area – one of the most difficult jobs in the world. Basically, means running a sport for your nation within which everyone else thinks they know better.

Y
Yellow card: The card shown by the referee to a player to indicate that the player has been cautioned and temporarily suspended – for when you've been bad, but not really bad. More Reggie Kray than Ronnie Kray.

LAWS OF THE GAME

THE GROUND

The playing surface must be safe. As laws go, it's a bit obvious. A safe pitch doesn't mean that it shouldn't have swords sticking out of the ground or serial killers painting the white lines as your team warms up. It means that it should be flat, with no holes and, importantly, no dog poo. Dog poo is a massive problem for local clubs and not just a reference to the standard of passing that you see from lower league half-backs, who probably should be playing in the front row but think they're an international scrum-half. As a rule, keep dog shit and sexual predators off the field and you'll be fine.

The permitted surface types are grass, sand, clay, snow or artificial turf. Yup, you heard that right. You can play on a pitch made from snow – and that doesn't mean a pitch in Colombia funded by Mr Escobar. Clay is also an appropriate surface, as is sand. Grass is, of course, the most obvious construct, and just to balance up the xenophobia, that doesn't mean a pitch in Wales funded by drug money from Howard Marks.

THE DIMENSIONS OF THE PLAYING AREA

The playing area is rectangular in shape – that's assuming that your groundsman doesn't have glaucoma or a drink problem.

Any variations to these dimensions must be approved by the relevant union – creating a 50-metre pitch because your pack is usually blowing out of its arse after 29 minutes isn't a valid excuse.

Where the length of the field of play is less than 100 metres, the distance between the 10-metre lines and 22-metre lines is reduced accordingly, which isn't necessarily a bad idea in any circumstances given that this would increase the number of tries scored and reduce box-kicks. Box-kicks are the Piers Morgan of rugby, they're there, but we wish they weren't.

Where the width of the playing area is less than 70 metres, the distance between the 15-metre lines is reduced accordingly – a seriously bad idea, because the gaps between defenders would become even narrower. This means that it would be easier to break down the composition of Donald Trump's tan than break the defensive line.

The perimeter area shouldn't be less than five metres wide where practicable – meaning that players don't smack their heads on advertising signs in professional rugby, or the knees/plastic hips of amateur supporters.

LINES

There are solid lines on the ground. The solid lines are on:

• **The dead-ball lines and touch-in-goal lines** – The lines that the ball bounces over when cocky outside-halves overkick the ball, yet blame the ground, wind or ball. Outside-halves are never to blame for anything.

• **The goal lines** – The try line. Where dreams are made and legends forged. Or where you drop the ball and never get picked again.

• **The 22-metre lines** – The domain of the drop-kick restart. Where outside-halves skilfully kick short or blast long, and where forwards pretend to take a quick tap and fool no one.

• **The halfway line** – Where the game starts and restarts.

Also, the position on the pitch where referees share humorous comments with the kick-taker. Humorous comments that supporters can't hear and the kickers don't seem to find that funny.

• **The touchlines** – Where lineouts are awarded and executed. And the demarcation between those who are playing the game and those who are not. Though this doesn't stop those on the sidelines, who haven't played rugby for 40 years, telling those on the field what to do.

There are solid lines on the ground. The solid lines are on:

• **Five metres from and parallel to each touchline** – The first line in from the touchline and the area that nervous wings treat like an 18th century hermitage and refuse to leave.

• **15 metres from and parallel to each touchline** – The area where outside-centres either make a fantastic tackle or get skinned.

• **10 metres from and parallel to each side of the halfway line** – The mark on the pitch where a laser beam triggers a switch in the scrum-half's head, forcing them to execute a box-kick.

• **Five metres from and parallel to each goal line** – The nearest line to the try line. When psychologists ask

Exeter supporters to go to their happy place, it's here they choose.

There's one line, 0.5 metres long, that intersects the centre of the halfway line. No one knows or cares what this is for.

GOAL POSTS AND CROSSBAR

When padding is attached to the goal posts, the distance from the goal line to the external edge of the padding must not exceed 0.3 metres – that's 30cm of padding, or to use another metric, a tight-head's gut.

FLAG POSTS

There are 14 flag posts with flags, each with a minimum height of 1.2 metres – that's more flags than some second-team squads have players.

One flag post is positioned at each intersection of the touch-in-goal lines and the goal lines and one at each intersection of the touch-in-goal lines and the dead-ball lines (eight flag posts in total). Bear in mind that some poor bastard has to collect these after the game, when everyone else is either having a warm shower or a cold beer.

One flag post is positioned in line with the 22-metre line and the halfway line on each side of the pitch, two metres outside the touchlines and within the playing enclosure (six flag posts in total). More fucking flags.

OBJECTIONS TO THE GROUND

Teams must inform the referee of any objections to the ground before the match starts – because doing it afterwards is absolutely pointless because everyone has gone home.

The referee will attempt to resolve the issues and won't start a match if any part of the ground is considered to be unsafe – for example, if there's dog shit, it will be removed. If a massive fracking sinkhole has appeared, it's game over.

LAWS OF THE GAME

THE BALL

The ball is oval and made of four panels – and its bounce is as trustworthy as a 1970s Conservative MP in a brothel.

It is similar in shape to an egg, which is why rugby is sometimes called egg-chasing, which is stupid because you can't chase an egg – it doesn't move. And even if it did and you did catch it, it would break, meaning that you couldn't score a try, as you can't have control nor exert downward pressure on a runny yolk. Humpty Dumpty is the nearest thing to an egg that you potentially chase, but he didn't exist as far as we know.

It weighs 410–460 grams – the same as a fuckload of drugs.

Smaller balls may be used for matches between young players – similar weight to a smaller cache of drugs.

The ball is made of leather or a suitable synthetic material. It may be treated to make it water resistant and easier to grip – the modern ball has changed dramatically since the 1980s. During this period, particularly in the cold winter months, kicking a ball 1mm away from the sweet spot resulted in instant paralysis and is one of the reasons why so many elderly people limp today.

Its air pressure at the start of play is 65.71–68.75 kilopascals, 0.67–0.70 kilograms per square centimetre or 9.5–10.0 pounds per square inch. That means it must be softer than, say, a prison door, but harder than, say, a toasted marshmallow.

Spare balls may be available during a match – if you can prise them from the substitute props, who are normally practising their goalkicking on the other pitch.

THE TEAMS

NUMBERS

Each team has no more than 15 players in the playing area during play – unless you're playing at a lower level where substitutions are chaos. You could easily be playing with 17 and no one would know.

A match organiser may authorise matches to be played with fewer than 15 players in each team – a godsend for second and third teams as hungover players who vomited on the bus trip to the ground can be left to recover on the back seat. At least until the drinking resumes on the trip back.

A team may make an objection to the referee about the number of players in their opponent's team. If a team has too many players, the referee orders the captain of that team to reduce the number appropriately. The score at the time of the objection remains unaltered – absolute chaos at times.

For international matches, a union may nominate up to eight replacements, or 'finishers' as they have become known now. 'Finishers' is a term unique to rugby and the porn industry. It has been suggested that all starting rugby players become known as fluffers, but as yet it has received a lukewarm response from players' associations.

For other matches, the match organiser decides how many replacements may be nominated, up to a maximum of eight. If you play second-team rugby and you have one replacement, you're doing well. If you need any more, merely put a shirt and shorts on any people or animals in the vicinity.

Replacements are made only when the ball is dead and only with the permission of the referee – unless you sneak on and no one notices.

If a player re-joins or a replacement joins the match without the referee's permission and the referee believes the player did so to gain an advantage, the player is guilty of misconduct – a penalty is the punishment for the team and a glaring look at the assistant referee, who quite frankly should be paying more attention and not chatting to his mates while leaning on the railings.

There are a minimum number of front-row players by squad size and the minimum replacement obligations. A match organiser may, having taken player welfare into account, amend the minimum number of front-row players in the squad and the minimum replacement obligations at defined levels of the game – basically, the bigger the squad, the more props you need. Also, please allow for more fuel on the bus.

Where the match organiser has determined squad sizes of 23 and a team is able to nominate only two front-row replacements, then that team may nominate only 22 players in their squad – backs for show, props for dough.

Prior to the match, each team must advise the appropriate match official of their front-row players and possible front-row replacements and which position(s) in the front row they can play. Only these players may play in the front row when the scrum is contested and only in their designated position(s) – usually pretty obvious, as they're the players who are either eating or about to eat.

A replacement front-row player may start the match in another position – occasionally happens when a hooker comes on in the back row. Never in the backs because that would be stupid.

It's a team's responsibility to ensure that all front-row players and front-row replacements are suitably trained and experienced – suitably trained is a loose term. If you're over 17 stone and can't button the collar on any of your shirts, you're in.

UNCONTESTED SCRUMS

Scrums will become uncontested if either team can't field a suitably trained front row or if the referee so orders – the game will then descend into rugby league, which for most union supporters is blasphemy. Hell will freeze over and for every uncontested scrum that occurs an angel will burn.

A match organiser may stipulate the conditions under which a game may start with uncontested scrums. If you're a match organiser this probably means something to you; if you're not, feel free to ignore it.

Uncontested scrums as a result of a sending off, temporary suspension or injury must be played with eight players per side. This means that you can't stick one player in the scrum and then have the rest glory hunting in midfield.

When a front-row player leaves the playing area, whether through injury or temporary or permanent suspension, the referee enquires at that time whether the team can continue with contested scrums. If the referee is informed that the team won't be able to contest the scrum, then the referee orders uncontested scrums. If the player returns or another front-row player comes on, then contested scrums may resume – bit complicated, essentially means that you must have enough suitably massive, competent lumps on the field to face the other set of massive, competent lumps. Availability of massive, competent lumps is key to the whole process.

In a squad of 23 players or at the discretion of the match organiser, a player whose departure has caused the referee to order uncontested scrums can't be replaced – this means that unscrupulous coaches can't cheat. Although we all know the ones who would. If you're one of those coaches and you're reading this, we mean you. You know who you are.

Only when no replacement front-row player is available is any other player permitted to play in the front row – usually giving a back-row forward a chance to get in the mixer, or a mouthy wing who thinks he's harder than he is. So that's basically every wing excluding Brian Lima.

If a front-row player is temporarily suspended and the team can't continue with contested scrums with players already on the field, then the team nominates another player to leave the playing area to enable an available front-row player to come on. The nominated player may not return until the period of suspension ends or to act as a replacement – this means that a back-row forward usually has to pay the price because a prop has collapsed like any share price that the author of this book has ever invested in.

If a front-row player is sent off and the team can't continue with contested scrums with players already on the field, then the team nominates another player to leave the playing area to enable an available front-row player to come on. The nominated player may act as a replacement. If only props thought about the repercussions of their actions. But they won't, and that's the tragedy.

REPLACEMENTS

Permanent Replacement

A player may be replaced if injured. An injured player may not return once replaced. A golden ticket for players at lower levels who simply don't fancy playing because it's too cold, or if they're a wing and have been forced to play second-row. Simply manufacture a convincing limp and off you go.

A player is deemed to be injured if at national representative level it's the opinion of a doctor that it would be inadvisable for the player to continue. You can also see doctors making these decisions in lower league rugby in and around West London, where virtually all the players are doctors by profession, or solictors/ lawyers. Meaning that the doctor players have to be very careful, otherwise they will be sued by the lawyer players.

In other matches, where a match organiser has given explicit permission, a player is deemed injured if it's the opinion of a medically trained person that it would be inadvisable for the player to continue. If a medical person isn't present, that player may be replaced if the referee agrees. If you can see bones sticking out of stuff etc., they go off.

The referee can decide (with or without medical advice) that it would be inadvisable for the player to continue. The referee orders that player to leave the playing area. For example, at lower league level, if a second-row had an iffy kebab the night before and has shat himself in the scrum, thereby leaving his number eight with a face curry.

The referee may also order an injured player to leave the playing area to be medically examined – this is a safety valve to ensure that an absolute psychopath doesn't try to play on with their head hanging off.

Permanent Replacement – Recognise and Remove
If at any point during a match, a player is concussed or has suspected concussion, that player must be immediately and permanently removed from the playing area. This process is known as 'Recognise and Remove', one of rugby's great improvements in recent

years and a clear separation from the amateur days where a comet could enter our atmosphere, smash a player on the temple, and that player still be allowed to play on.

Temporary Replacement – Blood Injury

When a player has a blood injury, that player leaves the field of play and may be temporarily replaced. The injured player returns to play as soon as the bleeding has been controlled and/or covered. If the player isn't available to return to the field of play within 15 minutes (actual time) of leaving the playing area, the replacement becomes permanent. For example, let's say you had a mute character in traditional pantomime costume, typically masked and dressed in a diamond-patterned costume; if that Harlequin had blood on its face, real blood or not, it would have to leave the field.

Temporary Replacement – Head Injury Assessment (HIA)

In matches that have been approved in advance by World Rugby for use of the HIA process, a player who requires an HIA:

  • Leaves the field of play; and
  • Is temporarily replaced (even if all the replacements

have been used). The game can't restart until the player who requires an HIA has been temporarily replaced. If the player isn't available to return to the field of play after 12 minutes (actual time) of leaving the playing area, the replacement becomes permanent – when this happens, someone who played in the 1980s must say the game has gone soft and also how policemen used to be taller and summers used to be longer.

Temporary Replacements – All
A temporary replacement can be temporarily replaced (even if all replacements have been used). If you say the word temporarily enough it almost becomes meaningless.

If a temporary replacement is injured, that player may also be replaced – it's that word temporary again.

If a temporary replacement is sent off, the originally replaced player isn't permitted to return to the playing area, except to comply with Law 3.19 or 3.20, and only if the player has been medically cleared to do so and does so within the required time of leaving the field of play – I never want to read or hear the word temporary again.

If the temporary replacement is temporarily suspended, the replaced player isn't permitted to return to the field of play until after the period of suspension, except to comply with the relevant law, and only if the player has been medically cleared to do so and does so within the required time of leaving the field of play – after you've got your head around this, have a crack at quantum theory.

If the time allowed for a temporary replacement elapses during half-time, the replacement shall become permanent unless the replaced player returns to the field of play immediately at the start of the second half – never seen this happen, so don't worry about it.

Tactical Replacements Joining the Match
Tactically replaced players may return to play only when replacing:
- An injured front-row player.
- A player with a blood injury.
- A player with a head injury.
- A player who has just been injured as a result of foul play (as verified by the match officials).

A very well-meaning set of laws usually abused by a team replacing a prop at some stage of the game.

Rolling Replacements
A match organiser may implement rolling tactical

replacements at defined levels of the game within its jurisdiction. The number of interchanges must not exceed 12. The administration and rules relating to rolling replacements are the responsibility of the match organiser – usually seen during pre-season friendlies, often associated with pools of vomit, tears and regret.

LAWS OF THE GAME

PLAYERS' CLOTHING

All items of clothing must comply with World Rugby Regulation 12 – the author of this book would also like to see this rule extended to off-field clothing and haircuts. This law would be vociferously applied in an around the hairdressers of Exeter.

A player wears a jersey, shorts and underwear, socks and boots. The sleeve of a jersey must extend at least halfway from the shoulder point to the elbow – thereby removing the possibility of a rugby vest, which is a positive for all concerned. No one wants to see a prop's bingo-wings.

Additional items are permitted. These are:

• Washable supports made of elasticated or compressible materials – once the domain of fitness instructors and 80s discos.

• Shin guards – mainly used by hookers, in both professions.

• Ankle supports worn under socks, not extending higher than one-third of the length of the shin and, if rigid, from material other than metal – often worn by props who have had more injured calves than a negligent dairy.

• Mitts (fingerless gloves) – beware that you'll have so much piss ripped out of you that you'll be dangerously dehydrated within seconds of leaving the changing room.

• Shoulder pads – once the chosen overgarment of 1980s women to ward off the unwanted touches of misogynistic business types, now the garment of players keen to avoid the clutches of blindside flankers.

• Mouth guard or dental protector – a vital piece of equipment that prevents people from the 21st century from looking like people from the 12th century. Can make you sound like you're from the 12th century, which is difficult when calling moves and/or speaking to the ref.

• Headgear – this doesn't include top hats, though it possibly should.

• Bandages, dressings, thin tape or other similar material – seen mainly on older players. The injury build-up over a ten-year career leads many to look like Tutankhamun.

• Goggles – should really be standard issue in the French lower leagues.

• Studs, including those of moulded rubber, on the soles of boots – or as they were known before 2000, back combs. Studs are the things that once made things that were offside, not offside anymore.

In addition, women may wear:

• Chest pads – for obvious reasons. Would also be desirable for many male outside-halves wishing to make up for the fact that they can only bench candy floss.

• Cotton blend long tights, with single inside leg seam under their shorts and socks – surprised that we don't see more players do this, men included. If it's good enough for the NFL, it's good enough for rugby.

• Headscarves, providing they don't cause a danger to the wearer or other players – on a serious note, it's measures like this that make women's rugby feel very inclusive.

A player may not wear:

• Any item contaminated by blood – one of the few

prejudicial laws that has kept serial killer participation numbers way down in recent years.

• Any sharp or abrasive item – again a major stumbling block in attracting the murderer market.

• Any items containing buckles, clips, rings, hinges, zippers, screws, bolts or rigid material or projection not otherwise permitted under this law – if you're keen on killing, this is starting to look like a witch-hunt.

• Jewellery – rumoured to be the main reason why Mr T failed to make the USA's squad in the late 80s.

• Gloves – although many players catch like they're wearing 14-ounce boxing gloves, often they're not. They simply can't catch or have a glandular problem.

• Shorts with padding sewn into them – making the Kim Kardashian look unattainable for the modern player.

• Any item that's normally permitted in law but, in the referee's opinion, is liable to cause injury – this includes scaffolding poles, angry dogs and door handles licked by Covid patients.

• Communication devices – you could argue that a mouth is a communication device, but their removal would rank as one of the most severe televised genocides that the sporting world has ever seen.

The referee has the power to decide at any time that part of a player's clothing is dangerous or illegal. In this case, the referee must order the player to remove the item. The player must not take part in the match until the item is removed or rendered harmless – for instance, if James Bond was playing and 20 minutes in one of his boots turns into nunchuks, they can be removed.

If, at an inspection before the match, a match official tells a player that an item banned under this law is being worn and the player is subsequently found to be wearing that item on the playing area, that player will be sent off for misconduct – often the case if an outside-half has a comfort blanket.

The referee must not allow any player to leave the playing area to change items of clothing, unless they're bloodstained – this can lead to a dangerous situation whereby a player, mid-game, doesn't feel that the shirt matches the hue of his boots and will deliberately punch himself in the nose just to maintain sartorial standards.

LAWS OF THE GAME

TIME

A match lasts no longer than 80 minutes (split into two halves, each of not more than 40 minutes plus time lost), unless the match organiser has authorised the playing of extra time in a drawn match within a knockout competition. Unless you're watching two teams repeatedly box-kick – then the normal space-time continuum is abandoned and 80 minutes feels like a long enough period for nasal drift to occur on water-dwelling mammals.

Half-time consists of an interval not exceeding 15 minutes as decided by the match organiser. During this time, the teams and match officials may leave the playing enclosure – wherein professional players take on fluids, nutrition and team tactics, while amateurs usually check Twitter or have a quick blast on a vape.

In non-international matches, the match organiser may decide to reduce the length of a match. If the match organiser doesn't decide, the teams agree on the length of a match. If they can't agree, the referee decides – if the game is so one-sided that it looks like a prison shower scene, it's possible to call it a day early and get into the bar sharpish.

The referee keeps the time but may delegate the duty to either or both assistant referees and/or an official timekeeper, in which case the referee signals to them any stoppage. In matches without an official timekeeper, if the referee is in doubt as to the correct time, the referee consults either or both of the assistant referees and may consult others, but only if the assistant referees can't help – sponsored by Timex.

The referee may stop play and allow time for:
• Player injury for up to one minute. If a player is seriously injured, the referee has the discretion to allow more than one minute for that player to be removed from the playing area – serious point, no jokes here.
• Consultation with other officials – grey area, allows refs to have a chat about anything if they want to.

Once the ball is already dead, the referee may allow time for:

• Replacement of players – with other players, not objects. Although you could replace a scrum-half with a small, loud, yappy dog and not cause too much of a discrepancy.

• Replacing or repairing players' clothing – this doesn't include the shortening of hems or the addition of sequins.

• Retying a bootlace – often executed by captains trying to run the clock down, or tired locks who need a breather because they run like giraffes with congenital birth defects.

• Retrieving the ball – from the stand, a river, or the colon of the inside centre who keeps repeatedly being sent down the channel.

A half ends when the ball becomes dead after time has expired, unless:

• A scrum, lineout or restart kick following a try or touchdown, awarded before time expired, hasn't been completed and the ball hasn't returned to open play. This includes when the scrum, lineout or restart kick is taken incorrectly.

• The referee awards a free kick or penalty.

• A penalty is kicked directly to touch without the ball first being tapped and without the ball touching another player.

• A try has been scored, in which case the referee allows time for the conversion to be taken.

In short, if something has happened, but there's still something else that needs to happen, it can.

A team scoring a try may attempt the conversion or may decline it:

• The decision to decline the conversion must be relayed by the try scorer to the referee by saying 'no kick' after the try is awarded – never happens. More likely to see a tight-head turn down a slice of Viennetta.

• Provided the conversion is attempted or declined before time elapses, the referee will award a restart kick – obvious.

• If the conversion is attempted, time is taken from the strike on the ball – you need the fucking hand speed of Bruce Lee on the stopwatch for this law to make any difference.

When weather conditions are exceptionally hot and/ or humid, the referee has the discretion to allow for a water break. This one-minute break should be taken midway through the half, after a score or when the ball is dead near the halfway line – this is when players tip water on their head and shake their hair like they're trying to attract L'Oreal as a sponsor.

The referee has the power to end or suspend the match at any time if the referee believes that it would be unsafe to continue – includes plagues of insects, earthquakes, boiling hot lava pouring on to the pitch and some twat with Covid on a licking rampage.

MATCH OFFICIALS

Principle

Every match is under the control of match officials, which consist of the referee and two touch judges or assistant referees – and everyone with a mouth in the crowd. Additional persons, as authorised by the match organisers, may include the reserve referee and/or reserve assistant referee, the television match official, the timekeeper, the match doctor, the team doctors, the non-playing members of the teams and the ball persons.

Assistant referees and touch judges are responsible for signalling touch, touch-in-goal and the success or otherwise of kicks at goal. In addition, assistant referees provide assistance as the referee directs, including the reporting of foul play. In all seriousness, it is the most difficult job in any sport. To the point where it is impossible to get everything 100%. Hat tip to all officials, at all levels.

Appointment of the Referee

The referee is appointed by the match organiser. If no referee has been appointed, the two teams agree upon a referee. If they can't agree, the home team appoints a referee – at local level this could be anyone or anything. But be careful when agreeing to refereeing a game. Initially everyone will be grateful, but within seconds they will aim all of their hate that has built up during their miserable lives at you. It's a living hell, with no positive outcome. Don't ask how the author of this book knows this.

If the referee is unable to complete the match, the referee's replacement is appointed according to the instructions of the match organiser. If the match organiser has given no instructions, the referee appoints a replacement. If the referee can't do so, the home team appoints a replacement.

See above. It can turn into a shitfest.

Duties of the Referee Before the Match

The referee organises the toss. One of the captains

tosses a coin and the other captain calls. The winner of the toss decides whether to kick off or to choose an end. If the winner of the toss decides to choose an end, the opponents must kick off and vice versa – an arm-wrestle or a quick game of 'knuckles' would also be good but hasn't yet been ratified by World Rugby.

The match officials must inspect the players' clothing and studs for conformity – a quick check to make sure the boots haven't got Samurai swords attached to the bottom and you're good to go.

Duties of the Referee During a Match

Within the playing enclosure:

• The referee is the sole judge of fact and of law during a match. The referee must apply the laws of the game fairly in every match – quite how they do this really is an achievement. There isn't a sport in the world that's as difficult to officiate as rugby. It's easier to stand in the middle of the Hadron Collider and catch a particle in your fucking teeth than ref the breakdown.

• The referee keeps the time. However, the match organiser may appoint a timekeeper, who will signify the end of each half – advisable not to give this responsibility to someone on the sideline who has a pint in their hand otherwise you'll be playing 60-minute halves and there'll be players puking all over the place.

• The referee keeps the score – bit obvious, but that's what rules are for, sorry, laws.

The referee permits access to the playing area for players and replacements when it's safe to do so – unless it's behind the posts where substitutes are allowed to do whatever they like. This includes creating a ridiculous scene when one of their team-mates scores a try and the substitutes run up and hug them like they're extras in a shitty American musical TV drama. Stop doing that for fuck's sake.

The referee gives permission for players to leave the playing area – a clear and sensible rule but one that makes you realise how few players ever leave the pitch to go to the toilet. Given that all mammals frequently urinate and pass faeces, it's strange that so few toilet breaks ever take place, particularly given the vast amount of food that tight-heads eat and the forces exerted on them in the scrum – they're basically shitting machines.

The Whistle
The referee carries a whistle and blows it:

• To indicate the beginning and the end of each half of the match.

• To stop play. The referee has the power to stop play at any time – with power-crazed referees this can lead to excessive whistling and leave supporters wondering whether they're indeed watching a rugby match or have travelled back to Amnesia House, Ibiza, in around 1991.

• To indicate a score or a touchdown.

• To caution or send off an offender and a second time when the penalty or penalty try is awarded.

• When the ball becomes dead, other than after a failed conversion kick.

• When the ball becomes unplayable.

• When a penalty, free kick or scrum is awarded.

• When it would be dangerous to let play continue or when it's suspected that a player is seriously injured.

All of which makes you wonder whether it would be better if the ref, at Test level, should replace the whistle with a more modern digital solution, allowing for a different sound for each offence. Injuries could be highlighted with a quick blast of an ambulance siren or the music from *Holby City*. When a try is scored Tony Bennett's 'The Good Life' could feature and any high tackles would be followed by *The Sopranos* theme tune.

The Ball Becomes Dead

The referee will deem the ball to be dead when:

- The ball is in touch or touch-in-goal.
- The ball is grounded in the in-goal area.
- A conversion has been attempted.
- A try, penalty or drop-goal has been scored.
- The ball or ball-carrier touches the dead-ball line or anything beyond it.
- The ball hits anything above the playing area.
- Or it's had a massive stroke and has blood pouring from the valve.

The Ball or Ball-Carrier Touches the Referee or Non-Player

If the ball or the ball-carrier touches the referee or other non-player and neither team gains an advantage, play continues. If either team gains an advantage in the field of play, a scrum is awarded to the team that last played the ball – a law made all the more entertaining, of course, if the ref is planted on their arse by a massive rampaging blindside.

If the ball-carrier touches the referee or other non-player in the in-goal area and either team gains an advantage:

- If the ball is in possession of an attacking player,

the referee awards a try where the contact took place – this is, of course, always followed by a chorus of the attacking team jeering at the ref like they're in a Broadway musical.

• If the ball is in possession of a defending player, the referee awards a touchdown where the contact took place.

Which does, of course, make you wonder whether the easiest way to avoid messing up behind your own try line is to run straight at the ref.

If the ball is touched by the referee or other non-player in the in-goal area, the referee judges what would have happened next and awards a try or a touchdown at the place where the contact took place. By non-player, this could, of course, refer to the dickhead substitutes who are roaming around willy-nilly behind the try line. If you were good enough to warrant being on the pitch, you would have been selected to play in the starting line-up. You weren't, so get your arse back on the bench. Unlike Victorian children, substitutes should be neither seen, nor heard.

The referee may consult with assistant referees about matters relating to their duties, the law relating to foul play and timekeeping, and may request assistance related to other aspects of the referee's duties – a key feature of the modern game. This is where you realise that assistant referees actually have voices and personalities, something for which they're often castigated. If you're a referee with a personality, some people will instantly take issue with you. These people are often very unhappy with their actual lives and wish they were involved in professional rugby but usually spend their days filling in spreadsheets.

The referee may alter a decision after a touch judge or an assistant referee has raised the flag to signal touch, touch-in-goal, or an assistant referee has signalled foul play – teamwork makes the dream work.

Duties of the Referee After a Match
The referee communicates the score to the teams and to the match organiser. The method of communication is up to the referee. Could be poetry, mime or semaphore.

If a player was sent off, the referee gives the match organiser a written report on the foul play infringement as soon as possible. In local amateur leagues this is usually one of the same three players every week – the local lunatics, who 500 years ago would have been permanently situated in the village stocks having stuff thrown at their heads.

There are two assistant referees or two touch judges for every match. Unless they have been appointed by or under the authority of the match organiser, each team provides a touch judge. At amateur level this offsets the cheating and creates a level playing field.

The match organiser may nominate a person to act as a replacement for the assistant referees or touch judges. This person is called the reserve touch judge or reserve assistant referee and is situated in the perimeter area. At amateur level this will usually be anyone who is left in the car park or hasn't started their fourth pint. Three pints is the cut-off for amateur assistant referees.

The referee has control over the assistant referees or touch judges. The referee may tell them what their duties are and may overrule their decisions. If a touch judge is unsatisfactory, the referee may ask that the touch judge be replaced. If the referee believes a touch judge is guilty of misconduct, the referee has the power to send the touch judge off and make a report to the match organiser. Other than watching world leaders jostle for position in front of the photographers at a UN summit, this is one of the greatest powerplays in the modern world. Watching a referee talk to his underlings is a joy, knowing that next week the same official will revert to the underling role. It's like prison, but with less shanks.

During the Match

There's one assistant referee or touch judge on each side of the ground. The assistant referee or touch judge remains in touch except when judging a kick at goal. When judging a kick at goal they stand in the in-goal area behind the goal posts – sounds simple, but you would be amazed how many times one assistant puts up their flag and the other doesn't.

An assistant referee may enter the playing area to report foul play. This may be done only at the next stoppage in play and when the referee allows – often met with suspicion from the referee as the assistant is moving on to their turf both literally and figuratively. It's like the New York Mafia circa 1930 but with flags, not Tommy guns.

Signals

Each assistant referee or touch judge carries a flag or something similar with which to signal decisions – a law that's surprisingly vague for rugby. At lower levels, a jumper, rugby shirt or pair of shorts is often used, although carrying a taser would bring a certain amount of authority and possibly increase the standard of behaviour at the lineout. However, it may negatively impact the straightness of lineout throws, depending on the voltage delivered into the hooker's back.

Signalling the result of kicks at goal:

• One assistant referee or touch judge stands at or behind each goal post. If the ball goes over the crossbar and between the posts, they raise their flag to indicate a goal – a true joy to behold. The vigour with which the flag is raised can only be matched by a child opening a Kinder Surprise.

Signalling touch:

• When the ball or the ball-carrier has gone into touch or touch-in-goal, the assistant referee or touch judge holds up their flag. At amateur level, the flag will be raised three to five metres short of where the ball crossed the line depending on whether the official is from the home or away team.

• The assistant referee or touch judge stands at the place of the throw and points to the team entitled to throw in – seems simple. But getting the hooker to stay in the same position is tricky. Much like a real hooker they will rarely stay in the same location.

When the ball is thrown in, the assistant referee or

touch judge lowers their flag, with the following exceptions:

• When the player throwing in puts any part of either foot in the field of play – more likely to see a tight-head on a treadmill.

• When the team not entitled to throw in has done so – usually a scrum-half merely testing the patience of everyone around them, as they have been doing since their mothers gave birth to them, something that those mothers probably regret on a daily basis. The same can't be said of fly-halves' mothers, who should be, and are, very proud.

• When, at a quick throw, the ball that went into touch is replaced by another ball or, after it went into touch, it was touched by anyone except the ball-carrier who took it into touch or the player who is taking the throw. This is the domain of the ball boy/girl, who already has questionable ethics at an early age. Any ball boy/girl who deliberately tries to touch the ball, therefore preventing a quick lineout for the opposition, will usually present criminal tendencies later in life and will be jailed by their late teens.

• It's for the referee, and not the assistant referee or touch judge, to decide whether the ball was thrown in from the correct place – an interesting and strange responsibility for the referee, who already has more on their plate than a tight-head at a wedding.

Signalling foul play:

• A match organiser may give authority to the assistant referee to signal for foul play but this will inevitably annoy the referee, whose powerbase is dwindling faster than a Lib Dem.

• An assistant referee signals that foul play or misconduct has been seen by holding their flag horizontally and pointing infield at right angles to the touchline. In a world where we're taught that it's rude to point, this is an ugly side of rugby that's rarely talked about.

• If an assistant referee signals foul play, the assistant referee stays in touch and continues to carry out all the other duties until the next stoppage in play – essentially, just because you've spotted something beyond your pay grade, remember who you are. Stay on the line and keep waving the flag. You're not head of the house, or even the butler – now get back down to the kitchens where you belong.

• At the invitation of the referee, the assistant referee may then enter the playing area to report the offence to the referee. The referee will then take appropriate action – once called into the room by their parents, the child is allowed to speak. Must curtsy or bow on completion.

• If an assistant referee's verbal report to the referee leads to a player being sent off, the assistant referee submits a written report about the incident to the referec as soon as possible after the match and the referee provides it to the match organiser – this is real big boy/girl stuff, and where the assistant referee gets validated as a human being.

Additional Persons

Appropriately trained and accredited first-aid or immediate (pitch-side) care persons may enter the playing area to attend to injured players at any time it's safe to do so. Or, at amateur level, anyone with water or a sponge containing enough bacteria to mutate 4,000 viral strains in under 60 seconds.

The following may enter the playing area without the referee's permission, provided they don't interfere with play or make any comments to the match officials:

• Water-carriers during a stoppage in play for an injury to a player or when a try has been scored – because players get thirsty and also need instructions from control freak coaches.

• A person carrying a kicking tee after a team has

indicated they intend to kick at goal or when a try has been scored – because goalkickers need a kicking tee and also instructions from control freak coaches.

• The coaches attending to their teams at half-time – the point where control freak coaches get to exert said control.

Advantage

If a team gains an advantage following an infringement by their opponents, the referee may allow play to continue in an effort to keep the game flowing – often based on units of time and spatial measurement that are completely unique to that official and no one else in the known universe. Advantage can last for .5 seconds or up to a month.

METHODS AND POINTS VALUE OF SCORING

• **Try:** Five points – rugby's holy grail and increasingly hard to score, mainly due to Shaun Edwards. Much like penguins, these are seen more regularly in the southern hemisphere than the north.

• **Conversion:** Two points – rugby's pudding. Something sweet after the main. Often made difficult by selfish, lazy wingers with an attitude problem who dive over in the corner when they could run under the posts. It's why all outside-halves hate wingers and, according to a recent scientific survey, want them dead.

• **Penalty try:** Seven points – rugby's equivalent of a lottery win.

• **Penalty goal:** Three points – something that keeps the scoreboard ticking over and the reason goalkickers at professional level can afford posher cars than anyone else in the team. At amateur level, goalkickers will have a similar car, but more beer tokens in the clubhouse after.

• **Drop-goal:** Three points – one of the most difficult things to master in the world, not just rugby. This includes things like sequencing genomes.

DIFFERENT WAYS TO SCORE

Try

A try is scored when an attacking player:

• Is first to ground the ball in the opponents' in-goal. This is often by a showboating winger or, in recent years, a hooker – who have become the unsightly nouveau riche of try-scoring.

• Is first to ground the ball when a scrum, ruck or maul reaches the goal line – often by the number eight or a scrum-half sniffing around like a seagull on a kebab.

• With the ball is tackled short of the goal line and the player's momentum carries them in a continuous movement along the ground into the opponents' in-goal, and the player is first to ground the ball. Looks particularly good in the rain. Not so good on a synthetic surface where skin is removed and you end up looking like something from *Saw 3*.

- Is tackled near to the opponents' goal line and the player immediately reaches out and grounds the ball. One of the weirdest of rugby's laws, where despite having moved heaven and earth to get to the fucking try line in the first place, they make the last 6mm ridiculously complicated.

- Who is in touch or touch-in-goal, grounds the ball in the opponents' in-goal, provided the player isn't holding the ball – this law is like modern art. Makes sense to some, not to others.

Penalty Try

A penalty try is awarded between the goal posts if foul play by the opposing team prevents a probable try from being scored or being scored in a more advantageous position. A player guilty of this must be cautioned and temporarily suspended or sent off. No conversion is attempted. These are often a result of scrum domination, repeated sacking of mauls or if a player tries to make an interception. Thanks to the reckless play of many in the 1980s who deliberately slapped the ball down, future generations of potential interceptors are treated as modern-day criminals. Along with Margaret Thatcher, the recklessness of player slap-downs remains one of the blemishes of the 1980s.

Conversion, Penalty Goal and Drop-Goal

For any goal to be successful, the ball must be kicked over the crossbar and between the goal posts without first touching a team-mate or the ground – the opposite of soccer.

If the ball goes over the crossbar and over the height of the goal posts, the kick is successful if it's deemed that the ball would have gone between the goal posts had they been taller. Or we could simply make goal posts a bit bigger. They're already pretty big, so making them a bit bigger again is no biggie.

If the ball has crossed the crossbar and the wind blows it back into the field of play, the score stands – a pointless law you may think, unless you play the game in the west of Ireland.

Conversion

When a try is scored, it gives that team the right to attempt a conversion, which may be a place-kick or drop-kick. It's rare to see a drop-kick because it's so fucking difficult. Never trust a bouncing rugby ball. Ever.

The kicker:

• Uses the ball that was in play unless it's defective – or unless it was part of some flamboyant NFL-style celebration and bounced into an adjoining river. Has been known to happen at Gowerton RFC.

• Takes the kick in the field of play on a line through the place where the try was awarded, parallel to the touchlines – unless a scrum-half is taking the kick, then they will kick it from a place at least two metres nearer or on a better angle. Anything to cheat – those little bastards.

• Places the ball directly on the ground or on sand, sawdust or a kicking tee. The kicker may be assisted by a placer. Nothing else may be used to assist the kicker. It's rare to see anything other than a kicking tee these days. Gone are the good ol' days of mud and sand where the kicker also had to have a GCSE in pottery.

• Takes the kick within 90 seconds (playing time) from the time the try was awarded, even if the ball rolls over and has to be placed again – 90 seconds is a long time and has allowed certain kickers to develop pre-kick routines so elaborate that they could attract the sexual advances of a peacock.

The kicker's team, apart from a team-mate holding the ball, stay behind the ball when it's kicked and do nothing to mislead their opponents into charging too soon. Forwards stand on the halfway preparing for the next lifting pods. Scrum-halves use this time to think about who to irritate next.

If the ball falls over before the kicker begins the approach to kick, the referee permits the kicker to replace it. While the ball is replaced, the opponents remain behind their goal line – a further example of how untrustworthy rugby balls are. Even when placed in an object that's specifically designed to hold them, they can't be trusted. They're mini-Donald Trumps, but weirdly look less plasticky.

If the ball falls over after the kicker begins the approach to kick, the kicker may then kick or attempt a drop-goal – a goalkicker's worst nightmare where calm is replaced by bowel movements.

If the ball falls over and rolls away from the line through the place where the try was awarded and the kicker then kicks the ball over the crossbar, the conversion is successful – easier to understand particle physics.

If the ball falls over and rolls into touch after the kicker begins the approach to kick, the kick is disallowed – never fucking happened.

The Opposing Team at a Conversion
All opposing players retire to their goal line and do not overstep that line until the kicker begins the approach to kick. When the kicker does this, they may charge

or jump to prevent a goal but must not be physically supported by other players in these actions. This is the bit where all the players stand behind the posts and try to unify, but deep down they're all blaming the player who missed the tackle – usually a malnourished wing at lower levels.

The team must not shout during a conversion attempt. Nothing is mentioned about singing, and in a game of about 1 per cent margins this is surely something worth considering. How could a goalkicker concentrate when 15 players are singing? Also doesn't mention anything about rapping or beatboxing.

If the ball falls over after the kicker begins the approach to kick, the opponents may continue to charge – a joyous moment for any defender. It's like one of those nature documentaries where you see seagulls engulfing a hapless baby turtle.

If the opposition touches the ball and the kick is successful, the goal stands. Every coach encourages you to charge the ball down regardless. It is, of course, easy for them to say as they don't have to take a ball to the top of their frozen fingertips or, worse still, straight in the kisser.

Penalty Goal

A penalty goal can be scored only from a penalty – this is arguably the most unnecessary law in the book. It's so self-explanatory that it doesn't need writing down.

The kicking team must indicate their intention to kick for goal without delay – a wonderful loophole in the law that often catches the opposition off guard. Allows deceitful swines to pretend they're shaping for goal, not tell the referee officially, then cross-kick to the corner.

If the team indicates to the referee the intention to kick at goal, they must kick at goal. The intention to kick can be communicated to the referee or signalled by the arrival of the kicking tee or sand, or when the player makes a mark on the ground – vague and open to shenanigans. Happens at least once in every Six Nations.

The kick must be taken within 60 seconds (playing time) from the time the team indicated their intention to do so, even if the ball rolls over and has to be placed again – gives goalkickers plenty of time to line up the kick, perfect dance moves or perhaps boil an egg.

If the kicker indicates to the referee the intent to kick at goal, the opposing team must stand still with their hands by their sides from the time the kicker starts to approach to kick until the ball is kicked – never seen players stand with their hands by their sides. True enforcement of this law would make players look like Victorian schoolchildren. For this very reason, this law should be applied to the fullest.

If the kicker hasn't indicated an intention to kick at goal but takes a drop-kick and scores a goal, the goal stands – the lesser-spotted quick drop-goal. Only executed by teams who think they can win, with the clock running out, but they never do.

The kicker places the ball directly on the ground or on sand, sawdust or a kicking tee. The kicker may be assisted by a placer. Nothing else may be used to assist the kicker. If the kicker is to be assisted, it's usually by the player with the lowest IQ in the team, where the possibility of a boot to the head is neither a great worry nor to any future detriment.

Any player who intentionally touches the ball in an attempt to prevent a penalty goal being scored is illegally touching the ball – you're not allowed to charge down penalty kicks. This is a good excuse for a rest for many players, except for the winger who loves making a big song and dance when charging down kicks as it covers up other weaknesses in their game, such as catching, tackling and being able to handle more than four pints of Continental lager.

A defending player must not shout during a penalty kick at goal – this law is obviously in place to stop any shenanigans from the defensive team. It would be interesting to see if it was called into play should a defending player be stung by a bee, hit with a missile or shot by a local farmer's loose aim.

If the opposing team infringes while the kick is being taken but the kick at goal is successful, the goal stands, and a further penalty isn't awarded. If the kick is unsuccessful, the non-offending team is awarded a penalty ten metres in front of the original mark. Unlike a penalty in football, this could result in a penalty kick becoming harder as the angle narrows with every metre closer to the posts. You could in theory end up with a kicking angle similar to trying to kick an atom into an ant's anus.

Drop-Goal

A player scores a drop-goal by kicking a goal from a drop-kick in open play – and becomes an immediate legend to anyone who has attempted a drop-goal in open play. If the ball hits your foot, you've done well. If it goes forwards, you're eligible for the SAS. If it goes over the posts, you live tax free for ever in a country of your choice.

The team awarded a free kick (including where they opt for a scrum or lineout instead) can't score a drop-goal until the ball next becomes dead or until an opponent has played the ball, has touched it or has tackled the ball-carrier. Any such kick is deemed to be unsuccessful and play continues – just to make it even fucking harder.

LAWS OF THE GAME

FOUL PLAY

Principle

A player who commits foul play must either be cautioned or temporarily suspended or sent off – unless you play in the lower leagues in France, where you may be rewarded with a spring parade in your name.

Obstruction

When a player and an opponent are running for the ball, neither player may charge or push the other except shoulder to shoulder. Unless you're a prop involved in a kick-chase with a wing, in which case, knowing you're beaten, simply grab their shirt and halt their movement like a juvenile puppy on a training leash. The prop must then look at the ref and pretend that nothing has happened.

An offside player must not intentionally obstruct an opponent or interfere with play – often referred to as a lazy runner, which is an insult to lazy runners all over the world. Lazy runners merely sit on their sofa eating crisps when they should be out pounding the roads. They're not cheating openside flankers who know exactly what they're doing.

A player must not intentionally prevent an opponent from tackling or attempting to tackle the ball-carrier – this often transpires as a player slightly altering their line or leaning into the attempting tackler. For a clearer visual picture, just think of the 6.30pm train out of London Paddington. It's the same line you run when getting to the train doors. Head down, no eye contact and lift your elbows.

A player must not intentionally prevent an opponent from having the opportunity to play the ball, other than by competing for possession – that could mean literally fucking anything.

A ball-carrier must not intentionally run into an offside team-mate to obstruct the opposition – why they would do this no one knows. It may be a desperate search for the love and warmth of a team-mate. May point to a difficult childhood or recent relationship break-up.

A player must not obstruct or in any way interfere

with an opponent while the ball is dead – seems like one of the more obvious laws, but such is life.

Unfair Play

A player must not:

• Intentionally infringe any law of the game – again, you wouldn't think this needed reiterating, but here we are again.

• Intentionally knock, place, push or throw the ball with arm or hand from the playing area. Usually the domain of full-backs who, when under pressure behind their try line, often slap the ball out on purpose but then make it look like it happened by accident. Cue the *EastEnders* music.

• Do anything that may lead the match officials to consider that an opponent has committed an infringement – essentially, don't act like a soccer player.

• Waste time – it could be argued that this applied to Wales throughout most of the early 1990s with regards to supporters' time, but it's difficult to prove.

Repeated Infringements

A team must not repeatedly commit the same offence – this doesn't apply to openside flankers. A player must not repeatedly infringe the laws – see above.

When different players of the same team repeatedly commit the same offence, the referee gives a general caution to the team, and if they then repeat the offence, the referee temporarily suspends the guilty player(s) – usually at the scrum or maul time. Often involves collapsing stuff. Often collapses any hopes of an entertaining match too.

Dangerous Play
Players must not do anything that's reckless or dangerous to others – selecting Mauro Bergamasco at scrum-half falls into this category.

A player must not physically or verbally abuse anyone. Physical abuse includes, but is not limited to, biting, punching, contact with the eye or eye area, striking with any part of the arm (including stiff-arm tackles), shoulder, head or knee(s), stamping, trampling, tripping or kicking – or if you played in the 1980s, the good ol' days.

A player must not tackle an opponent early, late or dangerously. Dangerous tackling includes, but is not limited to, tackling or attempting to tackle an opponent above the line of the shoulders even if the tackle starts below the line of the shoulders – easier to interpret modern art.

A player must not tackle an opponent who isn't in possession of the ball – unless it's your mate playing for the opposition, then you can give their ribs a little tickle.

Except in a scrum, ruck or maul, a player who isn't in possession of the ball must not hold, push, charge or obstruct an opponent not in possession of the ball – one of rugby's unenforceable laws. At any one point, there will be at least three players holding another player's shirt. More often than not it's a prop trying to stop anyone faster than them from moving forwards – which means anyone on the pitch.

A player must not charge or knock down an opponent carrying the ball without attempting to grasp that player. You must attempt to wrap your arms around the player. It doesn't have to be a full hug, as if you're thanking someone for dragging you out of a burning building. But it must at least look like a half-hearted hug, i.e. like you're hugging your mother-in-law.

A player must not tackle, charge, pull, push or grasp an opponent whose feet are off the ground – often seen when two full-backs enter the air like graceful seagulls, only to collide in mid-air like two poorly serviced Russian fighter planes.

A player must not lift an opponent off the ground and drop or drive that player so that their head and/or upper body make contact with the ground – otherwise known as the 'tip' or 'spear tackle'. Massive in the 1980s, but now loathed. It's the Sarah Ferguson of rugby.

Dangerous play in a scrum:

• The front row of a scrum must not form at a distance from its opponents and rush against them – but deep down they all want to. If you test the DNA of a front-row forward, they're 50 per cent human and 50 per cent Montana mountain goat.

• A front-row player must not pull an opponent – this is rather like wishing for world peace. Not happening.

• A front-row player must not intentionally lift an opponent off their feet or force the opponent upwards out of the scrum – it's part of who they are as people and who are we to stop them fulfilling their dreams?

• A front-row player must not intentionally collapse a scrum – it's why they wake up in the morning.

Dangerous play in a ruck or maul:

• A player must not charge into a ruck or maul. Charging includes any contact made without binding on to another player in the ruck or maul – if you've ever seen a modern rugby match, you'll wonder whether the rule has been included just to make up a predetermined word count.

• A player must not make contact with an opponent above the line of the shoulders – very similar to drink-driving. A few decades back it was still illegal but not really enforced. Now, thankfully, both are taken seriously.

• A player must not intentionally collapse a ruck or a maul – unless they just feel like it.

A player must not retaliate – the restraint of modern professional players is remarkable. In the amateur era, if you hadn't taken at least one punch to the face, you weren't doing it properly.

Teams must not use the 'cavalry charge' or 'flying wedge' – which is a shame. Although incredibly dangerous, it turned rugby into an almost Roman spectacle – the sort of thing that you would expect to see at the Colosseum. In this instance, the solitary defender on the try line was the Christians, and the massive mass of flying flesh were the bloodthirsty lions.

A player must not attempt to kick the ball from the hands of the ball-carrier – a very sensible rule, sorry law. This stops locks from coming through the middle of rucks and sweeping their long uncontrollable legs at the ball, with the result being the scrum-half taking a boot in the face. Unless you're John Eales, no locks should be allowed to kick or swing their legs above knee height – on or off the field.

A ball-carrier is permitted to hand-off an opponent provided excessive force isn't used – one of the greatest parts of the game, and one that not only defeats a defender but also removes their confidence and eventually their soul. If a number eight hands off an outside-half, then the damage can be undone by two tries scored in the next match. If a number eight is handed off by an outside-half, that player must be placed in a witness protection scheme.

In open play, any player may lift or support a team-mate. Players who do so must lower that player to the ground safely as soon as the ball is won by either team. We're all used to seeing players being lifted at the lineout, but why have we not seen players being lifted for cross-field kicks or even to collect box-kicks?*

* *The author writes and thinks about rugby too much and, as such, these opinions should be ignored. Please take care not to watch too much rugby or you may end up as weird as him. Thanks, Polaris Publishing.*

Misconduct

A player must not do anything that's against the spirit of good sportsmanship – unlike those pitiful oafs in other sports.

Players must respect the authority of the referee. They must not dispute the referee's decisions. They must stop playing immediately when the referee blows the whistle to stop play – in all seriousness, this is one of the great aspects of rugby. Officials in many other sports must put up with all manner of abuse. It's this law that should be respected above all.

Yellow and Red Cards

When a player is being cautioned and suspended for ten minutes, the referee will show that player a yellow card. If that player later commits another yellow card offence, the player must be sent off. The author of this book would also like to see the introduction of a punishment involving a purple velvet glove, a limp slap across the face being issued for acts of total shithouseness such as gouging and biting. Revealing the purple glove would be the ultimate in dishonour.

When a player is being sent off, the referee will show that player a red card and the player will take no further part in the match. A player sent off may not be replaced

– a common occurrence in the modern game thanks to a necessary focus on player welfare and, in particular, high tackles. But prior to around the year 2000, you only received a red card if you removed someone's head, emerged from a maul with an eyeball in your hand or had enough skin on your studs for Ed Gein to make a new lampshade.

ONSIDE AND OFFSIDE

Principle

The game is played only by players who are onside –
you would be surprised at how untrue this statement is.

Offside and Onside in Open Play

A player is offside in open play if that player is in front
of a team-mate who is carrying the ball or who last
played it. An offside player must not interfere with
play. This includes:

• Playing the ball.

• Tackling the ball-carrier.

• Preventing the opposition from playing as they
wish.

The above laws alone gave birth to the sentence:
'Every time, ref.'

A player can be offside anywhere in the playing area. And will be, especially opensides, who spend more time on the wrong side of the law than those lovely people at Enron.

A player who receives an unintentional throw forward isn't offside – when reading this rule, some smartarse will usually say, 'Unless they're playing Super Rugby.'

An offside player may be penalised if that player:
- Interferes with play.
- Moves forwards towards the ball.
- Was in front of a team-mate who kicked the ball and fails to retire immediately behind an onside team-mate.

A player is accidentally offside if the player can't avoid being touched by the ball or by a team-mate who is carrying the ball. Only if the offending team gains an advantage should play stop – one of rugby's cruellest rules, sorry laws. Even Bruce Lee didn't have quick enough reaction times to avoid running into his man, a reason often cited for his limited game time in rugby and his decision to push on with his karate stuff.

Any offside player can be put onside when that player:

- Moves behind a team-mate who last played the ball.
- Moves behind a team-mate who is onside.
- Or they can stitch a number seven to their back and do whatever the fuck they want.

Other than under another complicated offside law, an offside player can be put onside when:
- An onside team-mate of that player moves past the offside player and is within or has re-entered the playing area.
- An opponent of that player:
- Carries the ball five metres.
- Passes the ball.
- Kicks the ball.
- Intentionally touches the ball without gaining possession of it.

Once you understand the above, can you please tweet me @thepaulwilliams and try to explain it to me. Cheers, Paul.

A player offside can't be put onside by any action of an opponent, apart from a charge-down.

Retiring from a Ruck, Maul, Scrum or Lineout

A player who is offside at a ruck, maul, scrum or lineout remains offside, even after the ruck, maul, scrum or lineout has ended. It's like being a 'rat' or a 'grass' in the underworld. Once you've been dubbed as such, you shall remain that for ever.

The player can be put onside only if:

• That player immediately retires behind the applicable offside line.

• An opposition player carries the ball five metres in any direction.

• An opposition player kicks the ball.

• Or they say they're an openside, then they're given keys to the city of Offside Land.

An offside player may be penalised if that player:

• Fails to retire without undue delay and benefits from being put onside in a more advantageous position.

• Interferes with play.

• Moves towards the ball.

• Or stays where they are, pleads ignorance and waves their hands around in the air like they're in a South American soap opera.

KNOCK-ON

A knock-on may occur anywhere in the playing area – but it's usually by a lock who has been released from his shackles and has strolled too near the touchline. If this happens, reshackle them to the ruck like they did to Sloth in *The Goonies*.

It's a knock-on when a player, in tackling or attempting to tackle an opponent, makes contact with the ball and the ball goes forward. One of rugby's most unfair rules. Quite how a player is supposed to tackle with the utmost aggression and use their arms while not occasionally knocking the ball forward is insane. Any knock-on from the tackle should be considered part of the tackle.

A player must not intentionally knock the ball forward with hand or arm. No reference to the head here, which opens up the possibility of the 'head pass'.

It isn't an intentional knock-on if, in the act of trying to catch the ball, the player knocks on, provided that there was a reasonable expectation that the player could gain possession. To avoid breaking this law always have the palms of your hands facing upwards like a Victorian street urchin begging for some extra gruel.

The ball isn't knocked on, and play continues, if:
• A player knocks the ball forward immediately after an opponent has kicked it (charge-down). Good news that it isn't a knock-on, bad news is you've probably broken your nose and snapped a couple of fingers.
• A player rips or knocks the ball from an opponent and the ball goes forward from the opponent's hand or arm. Think of it like flesh pinball.

Throw Forward
A throw forward may occur anywhere in the playing area. This is where you can make up your own cruel joke about that playing area being Super Rugby.

A player must not intentionally throw or pass the ball forward. See above.

KICK-OFFS AND RESTARTS

Principle

Kick-offs are used to start each half of the match or period of extra time. Restart kicks resume play after a score or touchdown.

All kick-offs and restart kicks are drop-kicks. Only outside-halves and scrum-halves are usually trusted with this responsibility. If you ever see a lock taking a restart, you've died and gone to second-row heaven or are in a coma.

Kick-offs and Restart Kicks Following a Score

Kick-offs are taken on or behind the centre of the halfway line. Depending on the quality of the contact it will either be drilled low into the corner, floated beautifully above the 22-metre line or scuffed and fly through the air like a sock full of pus.

The opponents of the team who kicked off the match start the second half. Sharing is caring.

After a team has scored, their opponents restart play on or behind the centre of the halfway line. This always seems a bit unfair. If you've just conceded, surely you should get to receive possession next. Other than Brian O'Driscoll never winning world player of the year and Peter Kay refusing to make a third series of *Phoenix Nights*, this is one of the world's true injustices.

When the ball is kicked:

• Team-mates of the kicker must be behind the ball – rarely enforced. When it is, the blame is often aimed at a winger – especially at lower levels. Their behaviour at restarts is reminiscent of a recalcitrant hound. Most amateur wingers are very much like greyhounds, the difference being that greyhounds have better catching percentages and don't have piss running down their legs when faced with a high ball/frisbee.

• Opposition players must be on or behind the 10-metre line. At amateur level those who are not confident at taking restarts will either move very deep or very shallow, especially when it's very cold/wet and the ball resembles a frozen baby seal.

The ball must reach the 10-metre line – must, but often doesn't. When a kicker fails to clear the 10-metre line with a restart, their pack take it as a grave personal affront as they have often wasted nine metres of running, which many of them can ill afford.

If the ball reaches the 10-metre line but is then blown back or if an opponent plays the ball before it reaches the 10-metre line, play continues. Blown back is a rugby reference and not the title of a 1970s porno, although with rugby's desperate need for additional revenue streams, rugby porn films shouldn't be ruled out.

If the ball goes directly into touch, the non-kicking team chooses one of the following:
- The kick being retaken
- Scrum
- Lineout
- Quick throw

Once again, forwards will take great umbrage should this happen. Their revenge is often cold and cruel.

If the ball is kicked into the opponents' in-goal without touching any player and an opponent grounds the ball without delay or it goes dead through in-goal, the non-kicking team has the option of having the kick retaken or a scrum. The outside half will then pick up a blade of grass, throw it into the air and blame the kick on the conditions, not that they have duffed the kick, sending the ball on the same trajectory as a bag of fresh pasta.

If the ball is kicked into the kicking team's own in-goal and is made dead by a defending player or it goes dead through in-goal, the non-kicking team is awarded a five-metre scrum. Best experienced when the kicker has booted the ball into the back of one of his team-mate's heads from a 22-metre restart. Rarely witnessed but is possible due to the fact that many locks have heads the same size as commercial bins.

Restart Kicks Following a Touchdown (22-Metre Drop-out)

Apart from at a kick-off or restart kick, if the ball is played or taken into in-goal by an attacking player and is made dead by an opponent, play is restarted with a 22-metre drop-out. Then follows a great opportunity for a member of the tight five to show how good their long pass is, by ripping a long pass to the kicker, who is standing on the 22. Often seen in the lower leagues where it's common to find props who played their junior rugby as half-backs – it's a sad indictment on the high calorific intake of the Western world.

A 22-metre drop-out:

• Is taken anywhere on or behind the defending team's 22-metre line. Normally taken by a back, but often a fake drop-out will be attempted by a forward. Which fools no one, as their thighs are often so large that the inter-frictional forces make the motion of a drop-kick impossible.

• Must be taken without delay. There is, of course, always time for a few quick dummies of short drop-outs, of which the hooker will always be one.

• Must cross the 22-metre line. Almost impossible not to. You could drop a rugby ball on a spider's ankle and the ball would go forwards.

• Must not go directly into touch. But often can if the quality of shank is high enough.

An opponent must not charge over the 22-metre line before the ball is kicked. This law is aimed at hookers. They're aggressive and often prone to outbursts.

An opponent who is inside the kicker's 22 may not delay or obstruct the drop-out. Basically, if you're behind their 22, when the number ten is getting ready to kick, don't behave like a dickhead. This should be known as the 'scrum-half law'.

If the ball crosses the 22-metre line but is then blown back, play continues. Opens up the possibility of teams using wind machines to aid this happening, or a scrum-half talking so much shit that the hot air forces the ball to stop in mid-air and move backwards. Like the Hindenburg, but without the casualties.

If the ball doesn't cross the 22-metre line, advantage may apply. As may mocking of the skill level of the kicker.

If a 22-metre drop-out reaches the opponents' in-goal without touching any player and an opponent grounds the ball without delay or it goes into touch-in-goal or on or over the dead-ball line, the non-kicking team has the option of having the kick retaken or a scrum. Can only really happen if the ground is icy or the kicker has been using PEDs since exiting the womb.

The team-mates of the kicker must be behind the ball when it's kicked. Those who are in front of the ball when it's kicked may be sanctioned unless they retire and don't interfere with play until they're put onside by the actions of a team-mate. Rarely enforced. As with all instances of 'being in front of the kicker' it's usually a hyperactive wing who has had too much tartrazine in his orange squash.

GOING TO GROUND

Principle

The game is played only by players who are on their feet. Absolute bollocks.

Players who go to ground to gather the ball or who go to ground with the ball must immediately:
- Get up with the ball; or
- Play (but not kick) the ball; or
- Release the ball.

Unless you're an openside. Laws on the ground don't seem to apply to them. It would be interesting to see whether other ground-based laws, outside of rugby, also don't apply to them. For instance, could an openside occupy land that belongs to a Native American tribe and begin drilling for oil without any ramifications? We shall probably never know.

Once the ball is played or released, players on the ground must immediately either move away from the ball or get up. Or pretend they can't move for some reason and just lie there like a piss-head covered in kebab. Usually, a lock who can't control their limbs, or sometimes a prop using their BMI as an excuse.

A player on the ground without the ball is out of the game and must:

• Allow opponents who are not on the ground to play or gain possession of the ball.

• Not play the ball.

• Not tackle or attempt to tackle an opponent.

• Or lie on their back like a turtle that's about to bake to death in the sun.

Players on their feet and without the ball must not fall on or over players on the ground who have the ball or who are near it. Usually lasts for about 0.5 of a second before the players on their feet buckle like a cheap flatpack nest of tables. More often than not a lock, as their legs are too long for humans.

TACKLING

Principle

A tackle can take place anywhere in the field of play. The actions of players involved in the tackle must ensure a fair contest and allow the ball to be available for play immediately. Tackling is one of the central tenets of rugby and always aimed at the opposition. But, at amateur level, a tackle between team-mates can also occur and it's usually seen in an off-field setting. While waiting to use a urinal is a common example and usually results in the player who was tackled spending the rest of the night covered in (and worrying about being covered in) their own piss. Another popular location for the off-field tackle is when waiting in the queue at a pub or for takeaway food. The takeaway-queue-tackle often involves the tackled player being hoyed over the counter and landing on the floor near the freshly cut salads and condiments.

Requirements for a Tackle

For a tackle to occur, the ball-carrier is held and brought to ground by one or more opponents. The finest exponents tend to be back-row forwards and inside-centres. With a few exceptions, outside-halves tend to be at the other end of the spectrum. Most of them were born timorous and are uncomfortable when spending long periods of time away from their mothers.

Being brought to ground means that the ball-carrier is lying, sitting or has at least one knee on the ground or on another player who is on the ground. It's essentially like a game of Twister, but with massive people trying to get a bit of you to touch the floor.

Being held means that a tackler must continue holding the ball-carrier until the ball-carrier is on the ground. Ankle taps might look cool but they're largely pointless. Much like when you see a man in his forties riding a BMX.

Players in a Tackle

Players in a tackle are the:
• Tackled player

• Tackler(s)

Others:
• Player(s) who hold the ball-carrier during a tackle but don't go to ground.
• Player(s) who arrive to contest possession in the tackle.
• Player(s) who are already on the ground.
• Those on the side-lines, and at home on the TV, screaming that they could have done a better job as they tuck into their fifth can of Strongbow.

Player Responsibilities
Tacklers must:
• Immediately release the ball and the ball-carrier after both players go to ground. Much like communism, this sounds like a great idea but never really works out that way.
• Immediately move away from the tackled player and from the ball or get up. See communism above.
• Be on their feet before attempting to play the ball. Easier said than done if you're a second row. It's like watching a new-born giraffe exit its mother's womb and then take its first steps.
• Allow the tackled player to release or play the ball.

Depending on the mood of the openside flanker, this may or may not happen. If you catch them on bad day, it's like trying to get a pothead to let go of their Monster Munch.

• Allow the tackled player to move away from the ball. Never happens. The tackled player is often held in place by multiple players as they try to win a penalty for the carrier not rolling away. Easier to separate a six-month-old box of Sugar Puffs.

• Tacklers may play the ball from the direction of their own goal line provided they have complied with the above responsibilities and a ruck hasn't formed. Or pretend it's the 60s, at Woodstock, and do what the fuck they like.

Tackled players must immediately:

• Make the ball available so that play can continue by releasing, passing or pushing the ball in any direction except forward. They may place the ball in any direction. Also known as the long or short 'plant'. Players with longer limbs are able to move the ball further away from their body. Scrum-halves are able to move it about 3mm away because they have arms like a T-Rex.

• Move away from the ball or get up. If it's a lock trying to get up, there may be a wildlife documentary crew near, marvelling at nature's ability for life to continue even in the face of physical deformity.

• Ensure that they don't lie on, over or near the ball to prevent opposition players from gaining possession of it. Back when old-school rucking was allowed, this law was never required.

Other players must:

• Remain on their feet and release the ball and the ball-carrier immediately.

• Remain on their feet when they play the ball.

• Arrive at the tackle from the direction of their own goal line before playing the ball.

• Not play the ball or attempt to tackle an opponent while on the ground near the tackle.

Quite how the referee is supposed to see and process all of this is insane and really shows how difficult a referee's job is. Just the tackle area alone requires a minimum of four sets of eyes to see everything that's happening simultaneously. And despite many reports of people with four sets of eyes being spotted in various locations in South-West Wales, none have successfully passed the referee exams.

Any player who gains possession of the ball:

• Must play it immediately, by moving away or by passing or kicking the ball.

• Must remain on their feet and not go to ground at or near the tackle unless tackled by the opposition.

• May be tackled, provided the tackler does so from the direction of their own goal line.

• Or when the ball is stolen from the opposition, that player can emerge from the breakdown like a firefighter rescuing a baby from the ashes of a burning building. There are few greater sights in the game. See Sam Warburton's highlight reel.

Offside lines are created at a tackle when at least one player is on their feet and over the ball, which is on the ground. Each team's offside line runs parallel to the goal line through the hindmost point of any player in the tackle or on their feet over the ball. If that point is on or behind the goal line, the offside line for that team is the goal line. Don't worry too much about this rule, sorry law. No one else really does, so neither should you. You'll know if you're offside because someone will blow a whistle. Up until that point just keep doing what you're doing. It's much like stealing stationary from work – just keep going until someone notices.

The tackle ends when:

• A ruck is formed.

• A player on their feet from either team gains possession of the ball and moves away or passes or kicks the ball.

• The ball leaves the tackle area.

• The ball is unplayable. If there's doubt about which player didn't conform to the law, the referee orders a scrum. The throw is taken by the team moving forward prior to the stoppage or, if no team was moving forward, by the attacking team.

• Or when someone from the sidelines shouts, 'For fuck's sake ref, tackle's over.'

THE RUCK

Principle

The purpose of a ruck is to allow players to compete for the ball, which is on the ground. And for many second rows to take out the abuse they received as youngsters on the people in front of them in the ruck. All those years of hearing 'oi lanky!' or 'what's the weather like up there you massive fucking freak' can now be directed through the body of the opposition players. The greatest collision at the ruck often occurs when one formerly chastised lock meets another.

Forming a Ruck

A ruck can take place only in the field of play. Or potentially on the back of the bus on the trip home, especially if players have had a few pints.

A ruck is formed when at least one player from each team are in contact, on their feet and over the ball, which is on the ground. Sort of like mating but often with more bodily fluids exchanged.

Players involved in all stages of the ruck must have their heads and shoulders no lower than their hips. Very similar to the heads, shoulders, knees and toes song, the main difference being that if you do forget rugby's version, you'll be penalised, or worse still, cleaned out in a manner not seen since the New York Mafia was brought to heel.

Offside at a Ruck

Each team has an offside line that runs parallel to the goal line through the hindmost point of any ruck participant. If that point is on or behind the goal line, the offside line for that team is the goal line. This is rugby's version of a foot fetish and it can deliver very similar levels of enthusiasm. You'll regularly hear middle-aged men shouting, 'Back foot, ref!' at the referee. It's often unclear whether it's related to the game or their desire to see the ref in high heels.

Joining a Ruck

An arriving player must be on their feet and join from

behind their offside line. Or not – depending on the level. Sometimes they're allowed to arrive like space shuttles re-entering the earth's orbit.

A player may join alongside but not in front of the hindmost player. It's rugby's version of queue jumping. Don't do it. No one likes a queue jumper, especially in a busy pub. Pub queue jumpers are arseholes.

A player must bind on to a team-mate or an opposition player. The bind must precede or be simultaneous with contact with any other part of the body. Rarely happens. Much like glue-sniffing, joyriding, and ram-raiding, this seems to have gone out of fashion in the late 1980s. It's a real shame when these traditional pastimes die out.

Players must join the ruck or retire behind their offside line immediately. It means you either get involved or back away. This is where you tend to find 'ruck inspectors'. Usually very tall and heavy players who look like monsters but are, deep down, terrified of contact. The author of this book falls into this category.

Players who have previously been part of the ruck may re-join the ruck, provided they do so from an onside position. This is rugby's version of recycling, except in this instance it will do little to reassure Greta Thunberg and may actually upset her further.

During a Ruck

Possession may be won either by rucking or by pushing the opposing team off the ball. Very rare to see this anymore. Rucks are now won by a quick steal. Years ago, rucks were won by swathes of forwards pouring over the ball like that scene in *Jurassic Park* where the dinosaurs nearly crush Sam Neill and the boy before hurdling over the tree.

Once a ruck has formed, no player may handle the ball unless they were able to get their hands on the ball before the ruck formed and stay on their feet. Very difficult to avoid handling the ball. Much like a Hollywood movie producer from the 1990s in that they're bound to touch something that they shouldn't at some point.

Players must endeavour to remain on their feet throughout the ruck. The word 'endeavour' is working harder than Donald Trump's hairdresser there.

All players in a ruck must be caught in or bound to it and not just alongside it. A wonderful sentiment. Nothing more.

Players may play the ball with their feet, provided they do so in a safe manner. This allows the more dexterous players to pull the ball back with their feet. Twenty years ago, playing the ball with your feet was also used to create Mondrian-style paintings on an opposition player's back should they fall on the wrong side of the ruck.

Players on the ground must attempt to move away from the ball and must not play the ball in the ruck or as it emerges. Incredibly difficult to do. Easier to make a prop walk past Greggs.

Players must not:

- Pick the ball up with their legs. This is a remarkable law. Before this law one can only presume most forwards crouched over the ball, knelt and picked up the ball with their thighs. Rather like an ostrich giving birth, but in reverse.

- Intentionally collapse a ruck or jump on top of it. Does occasionally happen in the lower leagues, and when it does, the 'ruck flop' is a wondrous sight.

- Intentionally step on another player. This is the one thing that older supporters yearn to see return to the game. Along with the death penalty, a return to the gold standard and taller policemen.

- Fall over the ball as it's coming out of a ruck. This law assumes that rugby players tend to fall a lot. And more than that, they do it on purpose. There are of course clowns playing the game, but not in the sense that they deliberately fall over the ball and then splash themselves in the face with a squirty daffodil.

• Kick, or attempt to kick, the ball out of a ruck. An important law that stops those with long legs simply kicking the ball and ruining the ruck. Mainly applies to second-row forwards. A similar, although unwritten law, prevents them from playing footsie with the bus driver when sat at the back.

• Return the ball into the ruck. Happens all the time in the modern game as scrum-halves prepare for box-kicks. It's the equivalent of picking up a sandwich at a buffet, squeezing it, smelling it and then putting it back on to the buffet. Scrum-halves do both, proving that they're a danger to society in any number of situations.

• Take any action to make opponents believe that the ruck has ended when it hasn't. This law has never really been taken to its full extreme, where forwards create an on-field PR team and bombard the opposition with press releases and catchy GIF-based social media campaigns, convincing them that the ruck is in fact over.

Ending a Ruck

When the ball has been clearly won by a team at the ruck and is available to be played, the referee calls 'use it', after which the ball must be played away from the ruck within five seconds. Scrum-halves of course ignore all of this and merely continuing setting up a 'ruck train' that's long enough to have handled all the coal required to fuel the great industrial age of the late 1800s.

The ruck ends and play continues when the ball leaves the ruck or when the ball in the ruck is on or over the goal line. Often catches teams out and allows the quick thinking to sneak around the goal-line ruck and score a try – like a seagull pouncing on a rissole.

The ruck ends when the ball becomes unplayable. If the referee decides that the ball will probably not emerge within a reasonable time, a scrum is awarded. Occasionally happens when the ball is stuck in a prop's skin fold. The ball is then removed, the skin fold cleaned and the game continues.

THE MAUL

Principle

The purpose of the maul is to allow players to compete for the ball, which is held off the ground. It's basically a flesh tank and a great opportunity for perverts to let rip.

Forming a Maul

A maul can take place only in the field of play. Or in a retail setting on Black Friday/when McDonald's brings back the McRib.

It consists of a ball-carrier and at least one player from each team bound together and on their feet. Just picture the last watermelon available in Tesco and two people who like watermelon really fancying some watermelon.

Once formed, a maul must move towards a goal line – sometimes at the speed of an alcoholic worm, other times at the speed of a normal worm.

Offside at a Maul

Each team has an offside line that runs parallel to the goal line through the maul participants' hindmost foot that's nearest to that team's goal line. If that foot is on or behind the goal line, the offside line for that team is the goal line. Another one for the foot fetishists out there. For a game that thrives on its separation from football, rugby mentions feet a lot.

A player must either join a maul from an onside position or retire behind their offside line immediately. Often impossible to spot. With a 16-man maul it's like watching squids make love.

Players who leave a maul must immediately retire behind the offside line. These players may re-join the maul. Never happens. Mauls mutate quicker than a coronavirus and are just as difficult to manage. A vaccination is currently being developed to stop players re-joining mauls incorrectly, but the data doesn't look too good at this stage.

Joining a Maul

Players joining a maul must:

- Do so from an onside position. Or pretend to.
- Bind on to the hindmost player in the maul. Or not, and then just slide up the side of the maul like a mollusc.
- Have their heads and shoulders no lower than their hips. This is, after all, a maul and not a scene from the tail end of the French Revolution.

During a Maul

The ball-carrier in a maul may go to ground provided that player makes the ball available immediately. Trickier than it sounds. Try falling to the ground with eight players holding you under the arms and around your head. Easier to sneak drugs into prison.

All other players in a maul must endeavour to stay on their feet. Very difficult to do. Adds an awful lot of weight to gravity. And gravity is already really heavy as it is. If there's one criticism of Newton's work, it's that he didn't fully explore how much weight a rugby player adds to one of the key forces in the universe. Some say Newton was too busy to worry about rugby, others have said he was just too busy eating fucking apples. We may never truly know.

All players in a maul must be caught in or bound to it and not just alongside it. Rugby BDSM at its finest.

Players must not:

• Intentionally collapse a maul or jump on top of it. Don't treat a maul like it's a bouncy castle. Despite the levels of body fat found at some level of the game, a maul isn't as bouncy as it would first appear.

• Attempt to drag an opponent out of a maul. You're not a bailiff on the fringes of the law, so don't act like one.

• Take any action to make opponents believe that the maul has ended when it hasn't. For instance, showing them Nostradamus's book and saying that he predicted this maul would be over very soon.

When players of the team who are not in possession of the ball intentionally leave the maul, such that there are no players of that team left in the maul, the maul continues. Not constrained by the opposition, the maul could theoretically spiral through space and time for eternity, possibly meeting an intelligent life form along the way, with that alien civilisation then believing that earth is populated with 320-stone masses of arms and legs that thrive in mud and love beer and pasties.

When all players of the team who are not in possession of the ball intentionally leave the maul, they may re-join provided that the first player binds on the frontmost player of the team in possession of the ball. Like an inverted conga, but with less music and far more pressure being exerted on your chest, neck and lungs.

When a maul has stopped moving towards a goal line for more than five seconds but the ball is being moved and the referee can see it, the referee instructs the players to use the ball. The team in possession must then use the ball within a reasonable time. The maul then becomes a flesh vending machine. The scum-half types in the numbers that he wants, some stuff jiggles about, then the ball pops out.

When a maul has stopped moving towards a goal line, it may restart moving towards a goal line providing it does so within five seconds. If it stops a second time but the ball is being moved and the referee can see it, the referee instructs the team to use the ball. The team in possession must then use the ball within a reasonable time. You get two chances essentially. Kind of like drug running in the way the goods are hidden and in the manner of punishment. First time, it's okay. Second time, someone blows the whistle.

THE MARK

Principle

A means of stopping play within a player's own 22 by directly catching an opponent's kick. Poor Mark. If this isn't bullying, I don't know what is. And one of the main reasons why there are so few great rugby players called Mark. Many start playing the sport with vigour, only to become nervous wrecks with their name being shouted regularly and in such an accusatory manner. Rugby is rightly a very inclusive game and is becoming more so each year. Unless you're a Mark. If you are, our sympathies go out to you.

Claiming a Mark

To claim a mark, a player must:

- Have at least one foot on or behind their own

22-metre line when catching the ball or when landing, having caught it in the air; and

• Catch a ball that has reached the plane of the 22-metre line directly from an opponent's kick before it touches the ground or another player; and

• Simultaneously call 'mark'. It's a lot to remember and difficult to execute for the uninitiated. Similar to 'The Moonwalk' – looks good if you pull it off. But if you don't, you'll look like a right dick.

A player may claim a mark even if the ball hits a goal post or crossbar before being caught. Very unlikely to happen. As soon as a rugby ball hits the posts all sense of logic breaks down on the field. A simple strike of a rugby ball on metal posts turns 30 reasonably composed humans into 30 kittens.

When a mark is called correctly, the referee immediately stops the game and awards a free kick to the team in possession. He then immediately walks over to anyone called Mark to offer them the number of a good counsellor.

A mark may not be claimed from a kick-off or a restart kick after a score. Good news for all you Marks out there.

Restarting Play After a Mark

The player who claimed the mark takes the free kick. A wonderful sight if the mark has been taken by a second-row as you get to witness them trying to send a signal from their brain, down two metres of nerve endings, to their feet. Or as often happens, they're instructed to quick-tap the ball and pass it to a player who has normal levels of hand-eye coordination. The second option is much like seeing a parent instructing their child to hand over chewing gum in case they choke to death.

If the player is unable to take the free kick within one minute, a scrum is awarded to the team in possession. It's rare. But it can take a minute, sometimes more, for the brain signals to reach the feet of locks. The time may also elapse if the outside-half is flirting with a supporter on the sidelines, or the scrum-half has started a fight with themself.

TOUCHLINES

Principle

The field of play has side boundaries known as touchlines. When play reaches a touchline, the ball is in touch and becomes dead. Also, at lower levels, some spectators may tell you what you're doing wrong when you're near the touchline. Best to stay away from them if possible.

Quick throws and lineouts are methods of restarting the game with a throw after the ball or ball-carrier has gone into touch. One of the founding principles of rugby and one of the differences between it and rugby league. For those unfamiliar with rugby league, much like the Normans, Romans and Vikings, they were an imperial force who raided Wales in the 1980s and stole everything they could get their hands on.

Touch or Touch-in-Goal

The ball is in touch or touch-in-goal when:

• The ball or ball-carrier touches the touchline, touch-in-goal line or anything beyond. For example, a wing spots a number eight in his channel, shits it and steps directly into touch.

• A player who is already touching the touchline, touch-in-goal line or anything beyond, catches or holds the ball.

If the ball has reached the plane of touch when it's caught, the catcher isn't deemed to have taken the ball into touch.

If the ball hasn't reached the plane of touch when it's caught or picked up, the catcher is deemed to have taken the ball into touch, regardless of whether the ball was in motion or stationary.

The 'plane of touch' may sound like an airline founded by nudists, but it isn't. Think of it more like a forcefield emanating up to space from the touchline on the ground. To continue the space theme, at lower levels of the game, some of the people standing near the touchline look a lot like the people from the bar scene in *Star Wars*.

The ball isn't in touch or touch-in-goal if:

• The ball reaches the plane of touch but is caught, knocked or kicked by a player who is in the playing area.

• A player jumps from within or outside the playing area and catches the ball, and then lands in the playing area, regardless of whether the ball reached the plane of touch. Presents a great opportunity for wings to do something flashy and stop a lineout from being conceded by standing outside the touchline and then diving athletically back into the field to catch the ball. It doesn't make up for the ten tackles that they have probably missed during that very game, but it looks cool.

• A player jumps from the playing area and knocks (or catches and releases) the ball back into the playing area, before landing in touch or touch-in-goal, regardless of whether the ball reached the plane of touch. Also a pretty cool sight but once again doesn't cover the fact that most wings are tackle-shy and that's why they're on the wing in the first place.

• A player who is in touch kicks or knocks the ball, but doesn't hold it, provided it hasn't reached the plane of touch.

THE LINEOUT

Quick Throw

A player who carries the ball into touch must release the ball immediately so that a quick throw may be taken. Even if the ball is released by the player who took it into touch, it must be thrown sneakily behind their back and on to the floor, like a weed dealer flicking drugs away in the presence of an arresting officer.

At a quick throw, the ball is thrown in:

• Between the mark of touch and the thrower's own goal line; and

• Parallel to or towards the thrower's own goal line; and

• So that it reaches the five-metre line before it touches the ground or hits a player; and

• By a player whose feet are both outside the field of play.

Often thrown in a short distance to a team-mate, but in its most glorious form thrown 20 metres over the heads of defenders straight to the full-back in midfield. The quick throw is vital at elite level to take advantage of broken defensive lines. At lower levels it can resemble something from the slapstick era of cinema, where varying people, in varying positions, of varying skill levels, merely throw the ball infield and then panic. They then continue to throw the ball around, like it's a handful of warm Ebola, while getting ever closer to their own try line.

A quick throw is disallowed and a lineout is awarded to the same team if:
• A lineout had already been formed.
• The ball had been touched after it went into touch by anyone other than the player throwing in or the player who carried the ball into touch.
• A different ball is used from the one that originally went into touch.

Unless you're Matthew Rees and Mike Phillips playing for Wales against Ireland in 2011 of course. Then you can use whatever ball is presented to you by the ball boy, take a quick throw, score a try and then go on to win the game. But it's all fine, no one in Ireland bears a grudge about the incident and it has never been mentioned since. Not once.

The ball must reach the five-metre line before it's played, and a player must not prevent the ball from travelling five metres. Not as easy as it sounds, especially if you're passing the ball to yourself. Plenty can go wrong when passing a ball forward to yourself, especially when their wing is usually flying towards you. Get it right and you're the hero, get it wrong and you'll either get walloped by the defenders or, worse still, knock it on – which is the equivalent of taking a shit with your clothes on.

If the mark of touch is outside the 22, the defending team may take the quick throw inside the 22 but is deemed to have taken the ball into the 22. This is a lot to remember and one of the reasons why forwards, at lower levels, are not allowed to take quick throw-ins. If they do, they're put before a committee of village elders, tried and then often pelted with fruit and vegetables in the village square. One early theory on why props became so heavy is that repeated skills-based rugby infringements led to more time in the stocks and they merely ate the fruit and vegetables, mid-air, while they were being hurled towards them. This doesn't appear in any rugby texts but has been passed on verbally by generations of rugby sages.

A lineout is formed on the mark of touch.
Each team forms a single line parallel to and half a metre from the mark of touch on their side of the lineout between the five-metre and 15-metre lines. The gap between the lines must be maintained until the ball is thrown in.

At the lineout, a gap must be maintained until the ball is thrown in. It never is. For some reason, up to 16 men or women from entirely different villages, towns and cities, whose express aim for 80 minutes is to beat each other in one way or another, refuse to be apart. It's like a weird Hollywood love story where, despite their differences, they can't be separated.

A minimum of two players from each team are required to form a lineout. Much like a marriage, this often ends in a mess, with both parties trying to grab hold of stuff that neither really owns.

Teams form the lineout without delay. After a five-minute team talk and the hooker has wiped the ball more thoroughly than one does a new-born lamb.

The team throwing in determines the maximum number of players that each team may have in the lineout. A level of administrative power not witnessed since the fall of Rome.

Unless the throw is taken as soon as the lineout is formed, the non-throwing team may not have more players (but may have fewer players) in the lineout than the throwing team. This often shows up the lack of basic maths ability in the general population. A particular worry with clubs based in and around London, where a number of players who by day manage massive hedge funds, can't accurately count to eight.

The non-throwing team must have a player between the touchline and the five-metre line. The player stands two metres from the mark of touch on their team's side of the lineout and two metres from the five-metre line. Sometimes the hooker, or these days often the weakest defender in the backline is moved there. If you're moved there from the outside backs it rather defeats the object as the opposition knows exactly what's happened and why you're there. It's like writing 'thick kid' on a child's T-shirt and expecting their day to pass without incident.

If a team elects to have a receiver, the receiver stands between the five-metre and the 15-metre lines, two metres away from their team-mates in the lineout. Each team may have only one receiver. Usually a scrum-half and preferably more than two metres away so that the team-mates can't hear all of the shit that they're talking.

Once the lineout is formed, players:

• From the team throwing in may not leave the lineout other than to change positions with other participating players.

• From the non-throwing team may leave the lineout only to ensure that they don't have more players than the opposition. It's a Guantanamo Bay-type situation. You must stay there for an unnamed period, for an unnamed reason. On the plus side, you don't have to wear an orange suit, unless you play for the Netherlands or a team whose marketing director got pissed up before deciding on the alternate strip.

Participating players may change places in the lineout before the ball is thrown. This part makes the lineout look like a culturally significant dance, the sort you would have seen as an explorer when first navigating the world in the mid-16th century.

Players in the lineout who are going to lift or support a team-mate jumping for the ball may pre-

grip that team-mate providing they don't grip below the shorts from behind or below the thighs from the front. A sexual conduct case waiting to happen. The arse is fine from behind, but thighs are the go-to from the front.

Players must not jump or be lifted or supported before the ball has left the hands of the player throwing in. Essentially, you can't lift a player into the air like a flesh Eiffel Tower and leave them there until you decide to throw in. Although it would make it easier for hookers, and especially those hookers who have converted from playing in the centre, as they often can't throw for shit.

Players must not make any contact with an opponent before the ball is thrown in. No phone calls, no text and no sliding into the DMs.

Throwing in to a Lineout
The player throwing in the ball stands on the mark of touch with both feet outside the field of play. The thrower must not step into the field of play until the ball has been thrown. Rarely spotted. Hookers tend to cross the line more than a 90s MP fiddling with their expenses.

The ball must:

• Be thrown in straight along the mark of touch and reach the five-metre line before it hits the ground or is played. Very difficult to achieve, especially in the wind. That any lineouts have ever been completed in Wellington or Galway is a miracle. If it hits the ground before the five-metre line, your hooker may have a substance abuse problem.

• Be thrown in without delay once the lineout is formed. Rarely happens. You can master quantum theory during this period.

The thrower must not pretend to throw the ball. Unless they're a converted centre because there's little else that their throwing can be described as.

Opposition players must not block the throw. Another law written specifically for scrum-halves. Not since the days of the Wild West has one group of people been responsible for such flagrant disregard for the law.

During a Lineout
The lineout commences once the ball leaves the hands of the thrower. Then all manner of shenanigans ensues. In the 1980s, elbows to the face and a knee in the kidneys were commonplace. Now that has been

replaced with a series of complex movements and timings that are reminiscent of CERN's Large Hadron Collider. If it goes to plan, something quite beautiful happens; if it doesn't, everything goes to shit. With one late lift, an iffy throw or a player totally forgetting why they're standing there, a modern lineout can look like a Swiss cuckoo clock, with things and people jutting out with no discernible pattern or purpose.

Once the lineout has commenced, the thrower and the thrower's immediate opponent may:

- Join the lineout. Lineouts are nothing if not inclusive.
- Retire to the offside line of the non-participating players of their own team. Never happens.
- Stay within five metres of the touchline. Or otherwise known as hiding from contact.
- Move to the receiver position if that position is empty. Or wish that they had never transitioned from playing in the centre because then they wouldn't have to put up with all this lineout bullshit every week and getting blamed because it's windy and the locks are too heavy to lift.

If those players move anywhere else, they're offside.

This only applies on the field of course. If they choose to move house, bank or broadband provider that's fine.

Once the lineout has commenced, any player in the lineout may:

• Compete for possession of the ball – doesn't happen anymore but used to in the amateur days when every player seemed to jump and lineouts looked like the shittest pinball machine ever invented.

• Catch or deflect the ball. A jumper may catch or deflect the ball with the outside arm only if they have both hands above their head. This stops players using their inside arm and jumping across the lineout like a confused salmon that confounded evolutionary theory.

• Lift or support a team-mate. Players who do so must lower that player to the ground safely as soon as the ball is won by either team. Depends on whether you win the ball. If you do, your team-mates will bring you down; if you don't, you're on your own and fall to the ground like a punctured weather balloon.

• Leave the lineout so as to be in a position to receive the ball, provided they remain within ten metres of the mark of touch and they keep moving until the lineout is over. Breakdancing is an acceptable form of 'keeping moving' but one that has never truly broken through in rugby.

• Grasp and bring an opponent in possession of the ball to ground, provided that the player isn't in the air. You can't use your arms as massive flesh chopsticks and pluck a player out of the air like Mr Miyagi toying with a fly.

Offside at a Lineout

All lineout players are onside if they remain on their side of the mark of touch until the ball has been thrown in and has touched a player or the ground. Getting them to line up correctly in the first place is another matter. It's like herding crack-addicted cats.

Players jumping for the ball who cross the mark of touch and don't catch the ball must immediately return to their own side. Rather like the queue at a carvery. You can have one go, but if you forget to get a Yorkshire pudding on your first attempt, you must go back to your original position before you have another go.

Until the ball is thrown in and has touched a player or the ground, the offside line for lineout players is the mark of touch. After that, their offside line is a line through the ball. This a rule created specifically for those players who have a degree in physics and a post-graduate qualification in cartography.

When a ruck or maul forms at the mark of touch, a participating player may either:
- Join the ruck or maul; or
- Retire to the offside line, which is the hindmost foot of that player's team in the ruck or maul. Or at lower levels, just jump on top until you get told off.

Once the ball has been thrown, a lineout player may move beyond the 15-metre line. If the ball doesn't go beyond the 15-metre line, the player must immediately return to the lineout. Like a flesh yo-yo.

Players not participating in the lineout must remain at least ten metres from the mark of touch on their own team's side or behind the goal line if this is nearer. If the ball is thrown in before a player is onside, the player won't be liable to sanction if the player immediately retires to the onside position. The player can't be put onside by the action of any other player. In this regard, lineouts should be treated like fireworks. Unless you really need to be at the business end of things, retreat to a safe distance, otherwise you may get hurt. This applies especially to skinny wings and mouthy full-backs.

Once the ball has been thrown in by a team-mate, players who are not participating in the lineout may move forward. If that occurs, then their opponents may also move forward. If the ball doesn't go beyond the 15-metre line, the players won't be liable to sanction if they immediately retire to their respective offside lines. Picture the tide going in and out.

Ending a Lineout

The lineout ends when:

- The ball or a player in possession of the ball:
  - leaves the lineout; or
  - enters the area between the touchline and the five-metre line; or
  - goes beyond the 15-metre line.
- A ruck or maul forms and all the feet of all the players in the ruck or maul move beyond the mark of touch.
- The ball becomes unplayable.

Often followed by a try in modern rugby if the lineout is on the five-metre line. It is easier to score a try from a five-metre maul than it is to start a row on Welsh rugby Twitter.

Other than by moving to the receiver position if

that position is empty, no lineout player may leave the lineout until it has ended. If the ending of the lineout occurs in your own half, it will likely be followed by a box-kick. Box-kicks are the jellyfish of rugby.

THE SCRUM

Principle

The purpose of a scrum is to restart play with a contest for possession after a minor infringement or stoppage. A real spectacle and another thing that separates rugby union from rugby league. League does have scrums, but it's more like watching two handfuls of cress being pushed together by your nan. In union, scrums matter, and without one, you're screwed. You can have the best back-row in the world, but without a scrum, they mean nothing. Unless you have a tight-head with a neck from which you can suspend a moon, and a back so stable that you could balance a plate of frozen Maltesers on it, you've got no chance.

Forming a Scrum

A scrum is formed in the scrum zone at a mark indicated by the referee. The 'scrum zone' is also a good name for a singles bar for 40-year-old rugby supporters.

The referee makes the mark to create the middle line of the scrum, which runs parallel to the goal lines. The mark is, of course, well-intentioned but getting nearly 2,000kg of meat to settle on that mark is another matter. Easier to stop an undersexed dog from skidding on a freshly laid parquet floor.

Teams must be ready to form the scrum within 30 seconds of the mark being made. More of a wish list than a law, this one. When referees write to rugby Santa in December, this is normally top of the list. Sadly, Santa has been unable to deliver on this wish on any Christmas during the professional era. It has led many referees to think that Santa is made up.

When both teams have 15 players, eight players from each team bind together in formation. Each team must have two props and one hooker in the front row and two locks in the second row. Three back-row players from each team complete the scrum. A truly joyous spectacle, especially in the cold, when steam rises from the bodies, creating the largest jacket potato in the world.

When a team is reduced to fewer than 15 for any reason, the number of players in each team in the scrum may be similarly reduced. Where a permitted reduction is made by one team, there's no requirement for the other team to make a similar reduction. However, a team must not have fewer than five players in the scrum. Pointless having five players in the scrum. You may as well stick some balsa wood in there.

The players in the scrum bind in the following way:

• The props bind to the hooker. Like Mafia bosses preparing for a photo. The hooker binds with both arms. This can be either over or under the arms of the props. For front rows who don't play together regularly, particularly at amateur level, this can lead to confusion about where the arms are going. It's a bit like teenagers on their first date in a cinema, but with less affection.

• The locks bind with the props immediately in front of them and with each other – by putting their heads very near their genitals. Far nearer than you would appreciate if you've never played in that position. Depending on the levels of cleanliness of your fellow team-mates, this can feel like you've stepped back into medieval England.

• All other players in the scrum bind on a lock's body with at least one arm. Like very skilful limpets, with exceptional jackaling skills, on the back of a large whale.

The two groups face each other, either side of and parallel to the middle line. Like a weapon-less war.

The two front rows stand not more than an arm's length apart with the hookers at the mark. Picture a dark foreboding alley in 1970s New York, with steam pouring from pores and mouths instead of drains.

Engagement

When both sides are square, stable and stationary, the referee calls 'crouch'. The front rows then adopt a crouched position if they haven't already done so. Their heads and shoulders are no lower than their hips, a position that's maintained for the duration of the scrum. As if bending over to vomit. Some of them do, depending on what they drank the night before.

The front rows crouch with their heads to the left of their immediate opponents', so that no player's head is touching the neck or shoulders of an opponent. Or in the 1980s by slamming their head straight into the opposition player's head to show them how tough they were. We now know that wasn't a great idea.

When both sides are square, stable and stationary, the referee calls 'bind'. It's as if the ref throws a metaphorical egg into the mixture to make it bind. Which wouldn't be advisable as all six players would then fight over the egg because they haven't eaten for three minutes.

• Each loose-head prop binds by placing the left arm inside the right arm of the opposing tight-head prop.

• Each tight-head prop binds by placing the right arm outside the left upper arm of the opposing loose-head prop.

• Each prop binds by gripping the back or side of their opponent's jersey.

• All players' binding is maintained for the duration of the scrum.

Imagine one of those group dances from polite 17th century British society where the men linked arms with the women. It's like that but with a far greater threat of violence, less kissing and very little chance of marrying into a richer family and increasing your standing in society. Unless you're playing in the south-west of England, where most players are from the landed gentry.

When both sides are square, stable and stationary, the referee calls 'set'. To continue with the cooking analogy, this is where the gelatine is added. This, of course, isn't possible because most props are vegetarian – are they fuck.

• Only then may the teams engage, completing the formation of the scrum and creating a tunnel into which the ball will be thrown – a tunnel so complicated to organise and maintain that's it comparable only to the one that passes beneath the English Channel.

• All players must be in position and ready to push forward. Unless you have one of those show pony number eights who's too busy pulling on the shorts of the second-row in what can only be described as prison bullying.

• Each front-row player must have both their feet on the ground, with their weight firmly on at least one foot. Best to spread the weight on two feet to avoid limbs snapping.

• Each hooker's feet must be in line with, or behind, the foremost foot of that team's props. Not so relevant anymore as hookers don't 'hook' as they did in the old days, to the point where some of the more profit-focused club owners have questioned whether hookers need to have their legs at all. The savings on food, socks, boots and transport cost being cited as a reason to cut hookers in half, quite literally.

Throw

The scrum-half chooses which side of the scrum to throw in the ball. More power for these already unstable megalomaniacs.

When both sides are square, stable and stationary, the scrum-half throws in the ball:
- From the chosen side.
- From outside the tunnel.
- Without delay.
- With a single forward movement.
- At a quick speed.
- Straight. The scrum-half may align their shoulder on the middle line of the scrum, thereby standing a shoulder-width closer to their side of the scrum.
- So that it first touches the ground inside the tunnel.

You've got more chance of winning the lottery while surviving a plane crash than any of this happening.

During a Scrum

The scrum begins when the ball leaves the hands of

the scrum-half, an act that's miracle enough. Getting a scrum-half to give up any of the limelight is a task in itself.

Only when the scrum begins may the teams push. Easier to keep a Covid denier in the house.

Possession may be gained by pushing the opposition backwards and off the ball. The true glory of a scrum. Military in its simplicity and beauty until a second-row pushes too hard and shits themselves. One reason why number eights are overly aggressive by nature. You would be too if you lived with the constant threat of a lock's shit hitting your eyes.

Players may push provided they do so straight and parallel to the ground. Not happening. Props will try to push in any direction while making it look like it's straight. See any of Salvador Dali's 'staircases' for an illustration.

Front-row players may gain possession by striking for the ball but only once the ball touches the ground in the tunnel. But using their nimble little legs. Try picturing large legs of Iberian ham, covered in hair, swinging from a hook.

A front-row player striking for the ball may do so with either foot but not both at the same time. Means you can't swing both of your legs while dangling off both of your prop's necks. Like asbestos in schools, it was very popular in the late 70s.

The hooker from the team that threw in the ball must strike for the ball. Or look like they are.

A front-row player must not intentionally kick the ball out of the tunnel from the direction it was thrown. The opposite of Amazon – you can't send it back the same way if you don't like it.

Any player within the scrum may play the ball but only with their feet or lower legs, and they must not lift the ball. Pretend you're in a lap dancing bar. No hands under any circumstances.

If a scrum collapses or if a player in the scrum is lifted or is forced upwards out of the scrum, the referee must blow the whistle immediately so that players stop pushing. One of the most difficult aspects of a prop's life is being squeezed out through the top of the scrum – that and not being able to wear anything with a collar.

When the scrum is stationary and the ball has been available at the back of the scrum for three to five seconds, the referee calls 'use it'. The team must then play the ball out of the scrum immediately. The point at which the scrum-half either passes, runs or kicks the ball. Or if the number eight has been a good boy, the scrum-half will let him have a run with the ball as a little treat.

Offside at a Scrum
Players remain onside for the duration of the scrum. This means outside-halves can apply more tan, while full-backs can chat to themselves because they're too far away from anyone to communicate without a megaphone.

Prior to the start of play in the scrum, the scrum-half of the team not throwing in the ball stands:
• On that team's side of the middle line next to the opposing scrum-half; or
• At least five metres behind the hindmost foot of their team's last player in the scrum and remains there until the completion of the scrum; or
• Right next to the opposition scrum-half, with his elbow in his kidneys. Either that or saying that he's had sex with all of the opposition scrum-half's family.

Once play in the scrum begins, the scrum-half of the team in possession has at least one foot level with or behind the ball. This means that the ball, in the scrum, dictates where the scrum-half must be – which they hate. They won't listen to anyone or anything. Without rugby, most scrum-halves would either be in jail or wearing a tag.

Once play in the scrum begins, the scrum-half of the team not in possession:
- Takes up a position with both feet behind the ball and close to the scrum but not in the space between the flanker and the number eight; or
- Permanently retires to a point on the offside line either at that team's hindmost foot; or
- Permanently retires at least five metres behind the hindmost foot; or
- Does what the fuck he likes.

All players not participating at the scrum remain at least five metres behind the hindmost foot of their team. Prevents backs from getting hurt by bigger, stronger people than themselves.

When the hindmost foot of a team is in the in-goal area or within five metres of that team's goal line, the offside line for that team's non-participants is the goal line. If you find yourself in this position you're in deep shit and things are going to get very difficult. This is like that scene in the *Shawshank Redemption*.

As soon as the scrum ends, offside lines no longer apply. It's like the end of Prohibition in America and everyone goes fucking mental.

Resetting a Scrum

When there's no infringement, the referee will stop play and reset the scrum if:

• The scrum-half throws in the ball and it comes out at either end of the tunnel.

• The scrum collapses or breaks up before it has otherwise ended.

• The scrum is wheeled through more than 90 degrees, so the middle line has passed beyond a position parallel to the touchline.

• Neither side wins possession.

• The ball is unintentionally kicked out of the tunnel. Exception: If the ball is repeatedly kicked out, the referee must treat this as intentional.

It is easier to conduct peace negotiations in the Middle East than referee a scrum. That a single scrum is ever completed defies statistical probability.

When a scrum is reset, the ball is thrown in by the team that previously threw it in. By which time so long will have elapsed that democracy will no longer be the principal system under which the world is controlled, evolution will have promoted rats to the top of the food chain, the earth will have lost roughly one-third of its habitable surface and the sun no longer shines. Donald Trump is now just a talking head plugged into a computer and the UK has re-joined Europe, and left again, at least three times.

Ending a Scrum
The scrum ends:

- When the ball comes out of the scrum in any direction except the tunnel.
- When the ball reaches the feet of the hindmost player and it's picked up by that player or is played by that team's scrum-half.
- When the number eight picks up the ball from the feet of a second-row player.
- When the referee blows the whistle for an infringement.
- When the ball in a scrum is on or over the goal line.
- Or when the referee has lost the will to exist and simply leaves to referee a football match. They may get sworn at or spat at refereeing the football match, but at least the rules are simple.

Dangerous Play and Restricted Practices in a Scrum

Dangerous play in a scrum includes:

• A front-row charging against the opposition.

• Pulling an opponent.

• Intentionally lifting an opponent off their feet or forcing them upwards out of the scrum.

• Intentionally collapsing a scrum.

• Intentionally falling or kneeling.

Also known as the dark arts. The corridor between the six front-row forwards is akin to an early Victorian alleyway lined with slums. Unusual smells pollute the air, bare flesh is visible on every corner and the threat of violence is ever-present. The only thing missing is the heavy presence of gin, unless this is a summer tour game at a lower league. Then, the presence of all manner of alcoholic perfumes will arrest your senses.

Other restricted practices at a scrum include:

• Falling on or over the ball immediately after it has emerged from the scrum. Unless you faint at the sight of a rare successful scrum.

• Scrum-half kicking the ball while it's in the scrum. Unruly bastards.

• Non-front-row player holding or pushing an

opponent. Usually an openside – they do stuff like that.

• Bringing the ball back into the scrum once it has left. This contravenes the ball's rights under the Human Rights Act. If the ball wishes to leave, it must be allowed to do so. If the rugby ball wishes to leave and give up rugby totally, or indeed become a football or a baseball, then it can.

• Non-front-row players playing the ball in the tunnel. Stops second rows, who could otherwise be part of a circus freakshow, from scooping the ball with their legs.

• Scrum-half attempting to make an opponent believe the ball is out of the scrum when it's not. There's no depth too low for people like this.

PENALTIES AND FREE KICKS

Principle

Penalties and free kicks are awarded to restart play after infringements. They're the main reason that rugby doesn't descend into an all-out battle. Without it, a rugby pitch would become the Roman Colosseum, with lions eating warriors – that's not the Johannesburg-based team playing Glasgow.

Location of a Penalty or Free Kick

The mark for a penalty or free kick must be in the field of play and be no closer than five metres from the goal line. Regardless, the scrum-half will move it a minimum of 12 inches forward.

A penalty or free kick is taken from where it's awarded or anywhere behind it on a line through the mark and parallel to the touchlines. When a penalty or free kick is taken at the wrong place, it must be retaken. Although, in all seriousness, the game would speed up significantly and allow more attacking space if the free kick could be taken from anywhere five metres to the left, right and behind of the ball, like a 'preferred lie' in golf.

Options at a Penalty or Free Kick

A team awarded a penalty or free kick may instead choose a scrum. An intriguing option given how fragile modern scrums are. Even with a dominant tight-head, opting for a scrum from a penalty is like going to Vegas and putting your house, car and kids on red.

A team awarded a penalty or free kick at a lineout may instead choose a lineout or a scrum at the same mark. That's like going back to Vegas the week after and putting the only thing remaining in your life, your dog, on black. Unless the lineout is five metres from the opposition's line – then attempting a maul-based try is as good as odds-on.

Taking a Penalty or Free Kick

A penalty or free kick must be taken without delay. The word delay is working very hard there. Some teams execute quickly. Others have a full board meeting, with a break for lunch.

Any player from the non-offending team may take it, other than for a free kick awarded for a mark. The law may say 'any', but that does unofficially exclude most forwards. Number eights and back-row forwards can, some hookers can too, but under no circumstances should a second-row execute a penalty or free kick. Their brain is too far away from their limbs and the synaptic delay causes problems.

The kicker must use the ball that was in play unless the referee decides it's defective. Slightly contentious law. Telling a ball that it's defective could affect its self-esteem, so tread carefully.

The kicker may punt, drop-kick or place-kick (other than for touch) the ball. Real chance for the outside-half (usually) to show off in front of their mates and any attractive supporters watching on the sidelines.

The kicker may kick the ball in any direction. Usually not backwards, unless playing on the west edge of Ireland, Wales or Scotland.

Other than the placer at a place-kick, the kicker's team must remain behind the ball until it has been kicked. A good opportunity for the rest of the team to take a breather and for the scrum-half to tell the captain that he should be taking the kicks, not the outside-half.

The ball must be kicked a visible distance. If the kicker is holding it, it must clearly leave the hands. If it's on the ground, it must clearly leave the mark. Once the kick has been successfully taken, the kicker may play the ball again. A weird law that makes quick-tap penalties difficult for less skilful players. A simple bounce of the chest would suffice and allows all players to become a threat from free kicks and penalties. Oooooooh, that was another serious bit.

Opposing Team at a Penalty or Free Kick

When a penalty or free kick is awarded, the opposing team must immediately retreat ten metres towards their own goal line or until they have reached their goal line if that's closer. While holding their hands up in the air like the innocently accused at a witch's trial in colonial America.

Even if the penalty or free kick is taken quickly and the kicker's team is playing the ball, opposing players must keep retreating the necessary distance. They may not take part in the game until they have done so. Never happens. Someone always sticks out a stray leg or grabs a shirt – especially at lower levels. Tendency for all players to somehow forget how to walk or run in a straight line and therefore avoid contact with the opposition. Players go from being in full control of their walking and running style to regressing to toddlers and running in all directions at the same time.

If it's taken so quickly that opponents have no opportunity to retreat, they won't be sanctioned for this. However, they may not take part in the game until they have retreated ten metres from the mark or until a team-mate who was ten metres from the mark has moved in front of them. This is another opportunity for players to lose control of their ability to run and walk like a normal human and instead make contact with everything in front of them like a messed-up atom. All done while looking directly at the ref.

The opposing team may not do anything to delay the kick or obstruct the kicker, including intentionally taking, throwing or kicking the ball out of reach of the team awarded the penalty. This where we see one of the rarest passes in the game. The reverse ball roll. You face the opposition player head on, then with the ball in one hand, roll it out of that hand, behind your back and let it roll approximately five metres away. Rarely coached.

Opposing Team at a Free Kick

As soon as the kicker initiates movement to kick, the opposing team may charge and try to prevent the free kick being taken by tackling the kicker or to block the kick. Careful which bits you move. Hair, eyelashes and fingers are okay. Feet and legs not so much. Had the film *Carry On Rugby* ever been conceived, a player with an erection could have invoked this law.

If the opposing team charge fairly and prevent the free kick being taken, the kick is disallowed. Play restarts with a scrum at the mark with the opposing team throwing in. The defending team's coach will be over the moon because they love a charge-down.

LAWS OF THE GAME

GROUNDING THE BALL

The ball can be grounded in the in-goal area:
- By holding it and touching the ground with it; or
- By pressing down on it with a hand or hands, arm or arms, or the front of the player's body from waist to neck. Sounds easy – is not. Trying to ground a ball when there are 15 people trying to stop you doing it is problematic. Many people think that grounding the ball is the icing on the cake, the jam in the doughnut, but it isn't. It isn't the end – it isn't even the beginning of the end. Many a dream has turned into a nightmare when grounding the ball.

Picking up a ball is not grounding it. A player may pick up the ball in the in-goal area and ground it elsewhere in that area. Strange that this needs clarification because picking up something is clearly the opposite of putting something down. But while we're playing a game of state the obvious, sheep are not cows, lemonade isn't a disease and clouds are not genitals.

An attacking player grounding the ball in the in-goal area scores a try. Glory, money, awards and a plentiful supply of sexual partners await.

When an attacking player holding the ball grounds the ball in the in-goal area and simultaneously makes contact with the touch-in-goal line or the dead-ball line (or anywhere beyond), a 22-metre drop-out is awarded to the defending team. This has led to another of nature's greatest sights – the 'inflight touchdown', where a player scores a try while their legs are in the air. It's right up there with seeing a whale breach, salmon swimming upstream and a tight-head at a wedding buffet.

When the ball-carrier grounds the ball in the in-goal area and simultaneously makes contact with the touchline (or the ground beyond), the ball is in touch in the field of play and a lineout is awarded to the opposition. An easier demonstration of the adage 'to not drag one's feet', there has never been.

A defending player grounding the ball in the in-goal area results in a touchdown. A law that conjures up images of a quantum leap of a rugby player transporting into the NFL, which would also incidentally be a dreadful idea for a film.

If a tackled player has momentum that carries them into their own in-goal area, they can make a touchdown. The one situation where rain improves the game of rugby. Without water on the pitch, sliding over the line can remove skin and dignity. With water, the slide into a try is a guaranteed way to make YouTube. If full-backs had been part of the game Streetfighter, the sliding finish would have been their finishing move.

A tackled player near their own goal line may reach out and ground the ball in the in-goal area to make a touchdown, provided it's done immediately. Like Indiana Jones with his hat, you get a one-kick crack at it. If you fail, in the rugby version, the try is disallowed. In the other instance you lose a large portion of your hand and probably bleed out on the floor.

If a player is in touch or touch-in-goal, they can make a touchdown or score a try by grounding the ball in the in-goal area provided they're not holding the ball. More likely to see a politician pass a polygraph.

If a tackled player is in the act of reaching out to ground the ball for a try or touchdown, players may pull the ball from the player's possession but must not kick or attempt to kick the ball. Means you can't dive in with your feet like some degenerate soccer player.

Ball Kicked Dead Through In-Goal
If a team kicks the ball through their opponents' in-goal from the field of play into touch-in-goal or on or over the dead-ball line, the defending team can choose:
• To have a drop-out anywhere on or behind the 22-metre line; or
• To have a scrum at the place where the ball was kicked.

Forwards then begin to resent the kicker and the extra calories that they have been forced to burn.

Defending Player in the In-Goal Area
If any part of a defending player is in the in-goal area, that player is considered to be in that in-goal area, provided they're not also in touch or on or over the dead-ball line.

If a player, who is in the in-goal area, catches or picks up a ball that's still in the field of play, that player has taken the ball into in-goal. From this point on panic begins to set in and your options are limited. You can either admit defeat and touch the ball down, attempt a rushed off-balance kick or run headlong into defenders like the last days of the Somme.

If a player who is on or beyond the dead-ball line or who is in touch-in-goal catches or picks up a ball within in-goal, that player has made the ball dead. A murder trial will then ensue.

Corner Flag Post

If the ball or ball-carrier touches a corner flag or corner flag post without otherwise being in touch or touch-in-goal, play continues unless the ball is grounded against the post. A big step forwards for corner flag posts in society. They were once the lepers of rugby and touching them was frowned upon. Thankfully, our more open society allows corner flag posts to be accepted as part of the community.

Ball Held Up In-Goal

When a player carrying the ball is held up in the in-goal area so that the player can't ground or play the ball, the ball is dead. Play restarts with a five-metre scrum in line with the place where the player was held up. The attacking team throws in. When failing to ground the ball, the disappointment in the attacker's face is often clear for all to see. It's like a child on Christmas day trying to open a present that has been wrapped in Kevlar.

Doubt About Grounding

If there's doubt about which team first grounded the ball in the in-goal area, play restarts with a five-metre scrum in line with the place where the ball was grounded. The attacking team throws in. Depending on the scrum-half selection they may still choose to box-kick it two metres.

SEVENS

Same sort of thing, but with fewer players.

TENS

Same sort of thing, with fewer players than 15s but more than sevens. It's the nine box of chicken nuggets.